# Contents

2

# Hungarian Chestnut Cake

**Servings:** 12 **Yield:** 1 -9 inch cake

## Ingredients

- ¾ pound whole chestnuts, drained
- ½ cup unsalted butter
- 4 tablespoons dark rum
- 10 (1 ounce) squares bittersweet chocolate, chopped
- 6 large eggs eggs
- ¼ teaspoon salt
- ½ cup white sugar
- 6 (1 ounce) squares bittersweet chocolate, chopped
- ½ cup heavy cream
- 1 tablespoon dark rum
- 8 eaches marrons glaces (candied chestnuts)
- 1 cup heavy cream, chilled
- 2 tablespoons white sugar
- 1 tablespoon dark rum
- ¾ cup chopped marrons glace (candied chestnuts)

## Directions

### Step 1

Preheat oven to 350 degrees F (175 degrees C). Line the bottom of a greased 9-inch springform pan with parchment paper. Then grease the parchment paper.

### Step 2

Separate the eggs.

### Step 3

In a food processor puree the chestnuts with the butter and the rum, scraping down the sides, until the mixture is smooth. Add the melted bittersweet chocolate and blend the mixture until it is combined well. With the motor running, add the yolks, 1 at a time, and transfer the mixture to a large bowl.

### Step 4

In a bowl with an electric mixer beat the whites with the salt until they hold soft peaks, add the sugar, a little at a time, beating, and beat the meringue until it holds stiff peaks.

### Step 5

Whisk about one fourth of the meringue into the chocolate mixture to lighten it and fold in the remaining meringue gently but thoroughly. Pour the batter into the prepared pan and smooth the top.

### Step 6

Bake the cake in the middle of a 350 degrees F (175 degrees C) oven for 45 to 55 minutes, or until a tester comes out with crumbs adhering to it and the top is cracked. Let the cake cool in the pan on a rack for 5 minutes, remove the side of the pan, and invert the cake onto another rack. Remove the bottom of the pan, invert the torte onto a rack, and let it cool completely. (The cake will fall as it cools.)

### Step 7

To Make Glaze: Put 6 ounces of the finely chopped chocolate in a small bowl, in a saucepan bring 1/2 cup of the cream to a boil, and pour it over the chocolate. Stir the mixture until the chocolate is melted and the glaze is smooth and stir in 1 tablespoon of the rum. Dip each candied chestnut halfway into the glaze to coat it partially, transfer the chestnuts to a foil-covered tray, and let them set.

### Step 8

Invert the cake onto a rack set on wax paper, pour the glaze over it, smoothing the glaze with a spatula and letting the excess drip down the side, and let the cake stand for 2 hours, or until the glaze is set. Transfer the cake carefully to a serving plate and garnish it with the coated chestnuts.

### Step 9

Make the whipped cream just before serving the cake: In a chilled bowl with chilled beaters beat the 1 cup heavy cream until it holds soft peaks, beat in the 2 tablespoons sugar and the 1 tablespoon rum, and beat the mixture until it holds stiff peaks. Fold in the chopped candied chestnuts. Serve the cake with the whipped cream.

### Nutrition Facts

### Per Serving:

530.3 calories; protein 6.8g 14% DV; carbohydrates 45.8g 15% DV; fat 34.1g 53% DV; cholesterol 155.7mg 52% DV; sodium 98.3mg 4% DV.

# Chocolate Yule Log

**Prep:** 50 mins **Cook:** 10 mins **Additional:** 2 hrs 30 mins **Total:** 3 hrs 30 mins **Servings:** 10 **Yield:** 1 13-inch Yule log

### Ingredients

### For the Filling:

- 1 ⅔ cups powdered sugar
- ½ cup butter, at room temperature
- 1 ½ tablespoons unsweetened cocoa powder

- 1 pinch salt
- 2 tablespoons coffee-flavored liqueur
- ⅓ cup mascarpone cheese

### For the Sponge Cake:

- 2 tablespoons melted butter
- ½ cup unsweetened cocoa powder
- ½ teaspoon kosher salt
- 2 tablespoons all-purpose flour
- 5 large eggs, at room temperature
- ⅔ cup white sugar
- ½ teaspoon vanilla
- 2 tablespoons powdered sugar, or as needed

**For the Ganache Frosting:**

- 1 cup heavy cream, boiling-hot
- 1 (8 ounce) package dark chocolate chips

**Directions**

**Step 1**

Whip powdered sugar, butter, cocoa powder, salt, and coffee liqueur together in the bowl of a stand mixer on high speed. Transfer buttercream into a separate bowl and add mascarpone cheese. Mix until combined; set aside.

**Step 2**

Preheat the oven to 400 degrees F (200 degrees C). Brush a little melted butter over a 13x18-inch rimmed sheet pan. Line pan with parchment paper and brush remaining melted butter on top.

**Step 3**

Combine cocoa powder, salt, and flour together in a bowl; whisk or sift to break up clumps.

**Step 4**

Place eggs in the clean bowl of your stand mixer. Add sugar and whip until fluffy, thick, and very light in color. Add 1/2 of the cocoa powder mixture and vanilla extract; mix on low speed for a few seconds. Beat in remaining cocoa mixture on low for a few seconds. Switch to high speed; stop once mixture is moistened but not fully blended. Pull off the whisk attachment and whisk batter with it until evenly blended.

**Step 5**

Pour batter onto the prepared sheet pan and spread out with a spatula, leaving some room around the edges. Tap pan on the counter to knock out the large bubbles.

**Step 6**

Bake in the preheated oven until top is dry and edges start to pull away from the sides, 8 to 10 minutes.

**Step 7**

Dust a clean kitchen towel with enough powdered sugar to cover an area slightly larger than the sponge cake. Remove cake from the oven. Run a knife around the edges of the pan. Sprinkle some powdered sugar over the top. Run a spatula under the parchment paper to make sure it's not stuck to the pan.

**Step 8**

Quickly flip pan on top of the sugared area to invert the cake. Remove parchment paper and dust cake with more powdered sugar. Gently roll cake up inside the towel; allow to cool for 15 minutes.

**Step 9**

Unroll cake and dollop buttercream on top, reserving some for later. Spread frosting to the edges. Roll cake up over the frosting, using the towel to lift it if needed. Sprinkle more powdered sugar on top. Wrap log in plastic wrap. Refrigerate until firm, about 2 hours.

**Step 10**

Combine chocolate chips and hot cream in a bowl. Let sit for 1 minute. Whisk until chocolate melts.

**Step 11**

Make an angled cut 3 inches from one end of the log. Place log on a parchment-lined sheet pan. Apply some buttercream to the angled slice and attach it to one side. Spread a layer of ganache all over the cake, except for the swirls. Refrigerate for 15 minutes to firm up ganache.

**Step 12**

Carve lines into the ganache using the tip of a knife to create the appearance of tree bark. Refrigerate until completely chilled before serving. Dust with cocoa powder and powdered sugar.

**Nutrition Facts**

**Per Serving:**

526.3 calories; protein 6.4g 13% DV; carbohydrates 55.7g 18% DV; fat 33.7g 52% DV; cholesterol 165.4mg 55% DV; sodium 245.4mg 10% DV.

# Cheesecake with Cranberry Glaze and Sugared Cranberries

**Prep:** 30 mins **Cook:** 50 mins **Additional:** 8 hrs 30 mins **Total:** 9 hrs 50 mins **Servings:** 10 **Yield:** 1 9-inch cheesecake

**Ingredients**

**Cheesecake:**

- 10 eaches digestive biscuits (such as McVitie's)
- 5 tablespoons butter, melted
- 2 tablespoons confectioners' sugar
- ⅛ teaspoon salt
- 2 (8 ounce) packages cream cheese, softened

- ¾ cup white sugar
- 3 large eggs
- ¼ cup sour cream
- 2 teaspoons vanilla extract
- 1 orange, zested

**Sugared Cranberries:**

- ⅓ cup white sugar
- ½ cup water

- 1 cup fresh cranberries
- ¼ cup white sugar

**Cranberry Glaze:**

- 1 cup fresh cranberries
- ¼ cup water
- 2 tablespoons white sugar
- ½ cup confectioners' sugar

- 1 tablespoon orange juice
- 1 ½ teaspoons light corn syrup
- ½ teaspoon vanilla extract
- ¼ teaspoon salt

**Directions**

**Step 1**

Preheat the oven to 375 degrees F (190 degrees C). Grease the sides of a 9-inch springform pan. Line the bottom with a circle of parchment paper.

**Step 2**

Crush biscuits into crumbs using a food processor. Stir crumbs, butter, confectioners' sugar, and salt together to make the crust. Press into the bottom of the pan. Rinse food processor and set aside for the cranberry glaze.

**Step 3**

Bake crust in the preheated oven until firm, 8 to 10 minutes. Remove the crust from the oven and reduce the temperature to 325 degrees F (165 degrees C). Let crust cool while making the filling.

**Step 4**

Beat cream cheese and sugar together until smooth. Add eggs, sour cream, vanilla, and orange zest. Mix until well combined, stopping to scrape the sides and bottom of the bowl. Spoon batter over the crust.

**Step 5**

Bake until the filling is set but still soft in the center, 30 to 40 minutes. Cool cheesecake to room temperature, about 30 minutes.

**Step 6**

While the cheesecake is cooling, combine 1/3 cup sugar and water in a small saucepan. Bring to a simmer over medium-low heat and stir until sugar is dissolved. Pour into a bowl and cool for 10 minutes. Add cranberries and stir to coat with syrup.

**Step 7**

Refrigerate cheesecake and syrup-coated cranberries, 8 hours to overnight.

**Step 8**

Line a rimmed baking sheet with parchment paper. Place 1/4 cup granulated sugar in a shallow bowl. Drain the cranberries, then roll them in the sugar. Place the sugared cranberries on the prepared baking sheet and allow to dry, 30 minutes to 1 hour.

**Step 9**

In the meantime, make the glaze. Combine cranberries, water, and sugar in a small saucepan. Simmer, crushing cranberries, until jammy, about 8 minutes. Let cool slightly. Transfer to the food processor; add confectioners' sugar, orange juice, corn syrup, vanilla, and salt. Process until smooth.

**Step 10**

Strain cranberry glaze through a fine-mesh sieve and discard solids. Pour over the cheesecake and smooth across the top with a small offset spatula. Garnish with sugared cranberries.

**Nutrition Facts**

**Per Serving:**

447.6 calories; protein 6.3g 13% DV; carbohydrates 48.2g 16% DV; fat 26.3g 41% DV; cholesterol 122.9mg 41% DV; sodium 368.9mg 15% DV.

# Christmas Wreath Cake

**Prep:** 30 mins **Cook:** 2 hrs **Additional:** 1 hr **Total:** 3 hrs 30 mins **Servings:** 16 **Yield:** 1 tube cake

### Ingredients

- 1 ½ cups raisins
- 1 cup red and green candied cherries
- ¾ cup dates, pitted and chopped
- ¾ cup candied pineapple, diced
- ¾ cup chopped walnuts
- ½ cup flaked coconut
- 3 cups all-purpose flour

- 1 teaspoon baking powder
- ½ teaspoon salt
- 1 cup butter
- 1 ¼ cups white sugar
- 1 teaspoon lemon zest
- 4 large eggs eggs
- 2 teaspoons lemon juice

## Directions

### Step 1

Preheat oven to 300 degrees F (150 degrees C). Line a tube pan with 2 layers of brown paper or parchment, and grease well.

### Step 2

In a large bowl, whisk together flour, baking powder, and salt. Mix in raisins, dates, cherries, pineapple, walnuts, and coconut. Stir until all fruit is coated.

### Step 3

In another large bowl, cream the butter with the white sugar. Add lemon rind, lemon juice, and eggs; mix well. Stir in fruit mixture. Spread batter into prepared pan.

### Step 4

Bake for 2 hours or until a tester comes out clean. Cool completely on a wire rack.

### Nutrition Facts

### Per Serving:

413 calories; protein 5.6g 11% DV; carbohydrates 62g 20% DV; fat 17.3g 27% DV; cholesterol 77mg 26% DV; sodium 221.4mg 9% DV.

# Eggnog Cheesecake

**Prep:** 30 mins **Cook:** 55 mins **Total:** 1 hr 25 mins **Servings:** 16 **Yield:** 1 9-inch cake

## Ingredients

- 1 cup graham cracker crumbs
- 2 tablespoons white sugar
- 3 tablespoons melted butter
- 3 (8 ounce) packages cream cheese, softened
- 1 cup white sugar
- 3 tablespoons all-purpose flour
- ¾ cup eggnog
- 2 large eggs eggs
- 2 tablespoons rum
- 1 pinch ground nutmeg

## Directions

### Step 1

Preheat oven to 325 degrees F (165 degrees C).

### Step 2

In a medium bowl combine graham cracker crumbs, 2 tablespoons sugar and butter. Press into the bottom of a 9 inch spring form pan.

**Step 3**

Bake in preheated oven for 10 minutes. Place on a wire rack to cool.

**Step 4**

Preheat oven to 425 degrees F (220 degrees C).

**Step 5**

In a food processor combine cream cheese, 1 cup sugar, flour and eggnog; process until smooth. Blend in eggs, rum and nutmeg. Pour mixture into cooled crust.

**Step 6**

Bake in preheated oven for 10 minutes.

**Step 7**

Reduce heat to 250 and bake for 45 minutes, or until center of cake is barely firm to the touch. Remove from the oven and immediately loosen cake from rim. Let cake cool completely before removing the rim.

**Nutrition Facts**

**Per Serving:**

277 calories; protein 5g 10% DV; carbohydrates 22g 7% DV; fat 18.9g 29% DV; cholesterol 82.2mg 27% DV; sodium 186.7mg 8% DV.

# Favorite Old Fashioned Gingerbread

**Prep:** 25 mins **Cook:** 1 hr **Additional:** 20 mins **Total:** 1 hr 45 mins **Servings:** 9 **Yield:** 1 9-inch square cake

**Ingredients**

- ½ cup white sugar
- ½ cup butter
- 1 egg
- 1 cup molasses
- 2 ½ cups all-purpose flour
- 1 ½ teaspoons baking soda

- 1 teaspoon ground cinnamon
- 1 teaspoon ground ginger
- ½ teaspoon ground cloves
- ½ teaspoon salt
- 1 cup hot water

## Directions

### Step 1

Preheat oven to 350 degrees F (175 degrees C). Grease and flour a 9-inch square pan.

### Step 2

In a large bowl, cream together the sugar and butter. Beat in the egg, and mix in the molasses.

### Step 3

In a bowl, sift together the flour, baking soda, salt, cinnamon, ginger, and cloves. Blend into the creamed mixture. Stir in the hot water. Pour into the prepared pan.

### Step 4

Bake 1 hour in the preheated oven, until a knife inserted in the center comes out clean. Allow to cool in pan before serving.

### Nutrition Facts

### Per Serving:

375.1 calories; protein 4.4g 9% DV; carbohydrates 65.3g 21% DV; fat 11.2g 17% DV; cholesterol 47.8mg 16% DV; sodium 434.7mg 17% DV.

# Gluten-Free Fruitcake

**Prep:** 40 mins **Cook:** 1 hr 30 mins **Additional:** 1 day **Total:** 1 day **Servings:** 12 **Yield:** 1 loaf cake

## Ingredients

- ¼ cup raisins
- ¼ cup golden raisins
- ¼ cup dried cranberries
- ¼ cup dried cherries
- 5 ½ fluid ounces spiced rum
- 1 orange, zested and juiced
- ½ cup brown rice flour
- ½ cup almond meal
- ⅓ cup potato starch
- ¼ cup tapioca starch
- 1 teaspoon ground cinnamon
- ½ teaspoon ground nutmeg
- ¼ teaspoon ground cloves
- ¼ teaspoon ground cardamom
- ¼ teaspoon ground ginger
- 1 teaspoon baking powder
- 6 dates dates, pitted and chopped
- 2 figs large dried figs, chopped
- ¼ cup candied mixed fruit, chopped
- ⅔ cup butter, at room temperature
- ½ cup raw cane sugar
- 1 teaspoon vanilla extract
- 2 large eggs eggs, at room temperature
- ½ cup unsweetened applesauce

- ¼ cup whole raw hazelnuts
- ¼ cup raw walnut halves
- ¼ cup raw pecan halves
- ¼ cup raw whole almonds
- 1 ounce candied mixed fruit slices
- 3 tablespoons cherry brandy liqueur

**Directions**

**Step 1**

Put raisins, golden raisins, cranberries, and cherries in a bowl. Pour rum and orange juice over the dried fruit. Set aside.

**Step 2**

Preheat the oven to 325 degrees F (165 degrees C). Butter a loaf pan.

**Step 3**

Whisk brown rice flour, almond meal, potato and tapioca starches, cinnamon, nutmeg, cloves, cardamom, and ginger together in a bowl. Set aside 3 tablespoons of this mixture. Add baking powder to the larger portion; mix well.

**Step 4**

Combine orange zest, dates, figs, and 1/4 cup candied fruit in a bowl. Sprinkle in 2 tablespoons of the reserved flour mixture and toss to coat.

**Step 5**

Beat butter and sugar together with an electric mixer until creamy. Mix in vanilla. Add eggs one by one, beating after each addition. Mix in applesauce.

**Step 6**

Drain the dried fruit, reserving the soaking liquid. Add drained fruit to the fig mixture and toss with remaining 1 tablespoon reserved flour mixture.

**Step 7**

Mix soaking liquid into the butter mixture. Gradually add flour, stirring just until combined; do not overmix. Fold in hazelnuts, walnut halves, and pecan halves.

**Step 8**

Pour batter into the prepared loaf pan. Decorate the top with almonds and candied fruit slices.

**Step 9**

Bake in the preheated oven for 1 hour. Reduce oven temperature to 290 degrees F (145 degrees C). Continue baking until browned on top and a toothpick inserted into the center comes out clean, about 30 minutes more.

## Step 10

Remove from oven and let cool for at least 15 minutes before removing from pan. Brush cherry brandy on top. Let cake rest 24 hours for best results.

**Nutrition Facts**

**Per Serving:**

401.4 calories; protein 5.1g 10% DV; carbohydrates 45g 15% DV; fat 20.4g 31% DV; cholesterol 58.1mg 19% DV; sodium 132.6mg 5% DV.

# Mini Christmas Cakes

**Prep:** 1 hr **Cook:** 1 hr 30 mins **Additional:** 1 week 5 days **Total:** 1 week 5 days **Servings:** 24 **Yield:** 24 christmas cakes

## Ingredients

### Cake:

- 3 cups dried currants
- 1 ¼ cups raisins
- 1 cup sultana raisins
- ½ cup candied red cherries, chopped
- 8 fluid ounces brandy
- grated zest of 1 large orange
- grated zest of 1 large lemon
- 1 cup unsalted butter, softened
- 2 tablespoons unsalted butter, softened

- 1 cup brown sugar
- 2 tablespoons brown sugar
- 3 large eggs, beaten
- 1 tablespoon molasses, or more to taste
- 1 cup all-purpose flour
- ½ cup self-rising flour
- ¼ cup ground almonds
- 2 teaspoons mixed spice
- ½ cup ground almonds

### Decoration:

- 6 tablespoons apricot jam
- 2 ½ (4 ounce) packages marzipan

- ½ (1 lb 8 oz) box white fondant
- 1 teaspoon blue food coloring

## Directions

## Step 1

Combine currants, raisins, sultana raisins, and candied cherries in a plastic container with a lid. Pour brandy over dried fruit; stir in orange and lemon zest. Close container and set aside to soak for 2 to 3 days. Stir or shake container every few hours as you remember.

## Step 2

Preheat oven to 275 degrees F (135 degrees C). Line a baking sheet with 24 cupcake cases or lightly grease 24 ramekins.

## Step 3

Combine 1 cup plus 2 tablespoons butter and 1 cup plus 2 tablespoons brown sugar in a bowl and beat with an electric mixer until well combined. Add eggs and molasses and beat well. Stir in all-purpose flour, self-rising flour, almonds, and mixed spice until well combined. Fold in almonds and soaked fruit; mix well. Spoon mixture into the prepared cases or ramekins.

## Step 4

Bake in the preheated oven on the center rack until a toothpick inserted in the middle of a cake comes out clean, about 90 minutes. Allow to cool in their cases.

## Step 5

Store in airtight tins or wrap them tightly in greaseproof paper and aluminum foil for at least 10 days before decorating.

## Step 6

Heat jam in the microwave for 10 seconds until warmed and brush onto each cake.

## Step 7

Roll out marzipan between 2 sheets of plastic wrap. Cut out circles with a round cookie cutter or a glass with the same diameter as the cakes. Arrange marzipan circles on top of the jam on each mini fruitcake. Store fruitcakes in an airtight container before finishing the final decoration, 8 hours to overnight.

## Step 8

Roll out white fondant between 2 sheets of plastic wrap and cut out circles with the same diameter as the cakes. Press a cookie stencil with a snowflake pattern onto the fondant circles. Color in the snowflake pattern with blue food coloring using a small brush and place on top of the marzipan layer. Repeat with remaining cakes.

**Nutrition Facts**

**Per Serving:**

421.9 calories; protein 4.8g 10% DV; carbohydrates 66.5g 21% DV; fat 14.2g 22% DV; cholesterol 46.1mg 15% DV; sodium 57.9mg 2% DV.

# Peppermint Cheesecake

**Prep:** 15 mins **Cook:** 13 mins **Additional:** 3 hrs 30 mins **Total:** 3 hrs 58 mins **Servings:** 8 **Yield:** 1 9-inch cheesecake

## Ingredients

- 1 cup chocolate cookie crumbs
- 3 tablespoons melted margarine
- 1 (.25 ounce) envelope unflavored gelatin
- ¼ cup cold water
- 2 (8 ounce) packages cream cheese
- ½ cup white sugar
- ½ cup milk
- ¼ cup crushed peppermint starlight candies
- 1 cup whipped cream
- 2 (1.55 ounce) bars milk chocolate candy bars, finely chopped

## Directions

### Step 1

Preheat oven to 350 degrees F (175 degrees C).

### Step 2

Stir cookie crumbs and margarine in a bowl until evenly moistened; press into the bottom of a 9-inch springform pan.

### Step 3

Bake in the preheated oven until lightly darkened, about 10 minutes. Remove from oven and cool to room temperature; about 30 minutes.

### Step 4

Stir gelatin and cold water in a small saucepan over low heat until gelatin dissolves completely, about 3 minutes.

### Step 5

Beat cream cheese and sugar with an electric mixer in a large bowl until smooth. Gradually add gelatin mixture, milk, and peppermint candy; mix until well-blended. Chill filling until thickened, about 2 hours.

### Step 6

Fold whipped cream and chocolate into filling. Pour filling into crust; chill until firm, about 1 hour.

**Nutrition Facts**

**Per Serving:**

458.1 calories; protein 7.5g 15% DV; carbohydrates 39.7g 13% DV; fat 30.7g 47% DV; cholesterol 71.3mg 24% DV; sodium 323.1mg 13% DV.

# Carrot Cake

**Prep:** 30 mins **Cook:** 1 hr **Additional:** 30 mins **Total:** 2 hrs **Servings:** 18 **Yield:** 1 - 9x13 inch cake

## Ingredients

### Cake:

- 4 large eggs eggs
- 1 ¼ cups vegetable oil
- 2 cups white sugar
- 2 teaspoons vanilla extract
- 2 cups all-purpose flour
- 2 teaspoons baking soda

- 2 teaspoons baking powder
- ½ teaspoon salt
- 2 teaspoons ground cinnamon
- 3 cups grated carrots
- 1 cup chopped pecans

### Frosting:

- ½ cup butter, softened
- 8 ounces cream cheese, softened
- 4 cups confectioners' sugar

- 1 teaspoon vanilla extract
- 1 cup chopped pecans

## Directions

### Step 1

Preheat oven to 350 degrees F (175 degrees C). Grease and flour a 9x13 inch pan.

### Step 2

In a large bowl, beat together eggs, oil, white sugar and 2 teaspoons vanilla. Mix in flour, baking soda, baking powder, salt and cinnamon. Stir in carrots. Fold in pecans. Pour into prepared pan.

### Step 3

Bake in the preheated oven for 40 to 50 minutes, or until a toothpick inserted into the center of the cake comes out clean. Let cool in pan for 10 minutes, then turn out onto a wire rack and cool completely.

### Step 4

To Make Frosting: In a medium bowl, combine butter, cream cheese, confectioners' sugar and 1 teaspoon vanilla. Beat until the mixture is smooth and creamy. Stir in chopped pecans. Frost the cooled cake.

**Nutrition Facts**

**Per Serving:**

574.6 calories; protein 5.1g 10% DV; carbohydrates 63.7g 21% DV; fat 34.8g 54% DV; cholesterol 68.8mg 23% DV; sodium 347.2mg 14% DV.

# Double Layer Pumpkin Cheesecake

**Prep:** 30 mins **Cook:** 40 mins **Additional:** 3 hrs **Total:** 4 hrs 10 mins **Servings:** 8 **Yield:** 8 servings

## Ingredients

- 2 (8 ounce) packages cream cheese, softened
- ½ cup white sugar
- ½ teaspoon vanilla extract
- 2 large eggs eggs
- 1 (9 inch) prepared graham cracker crust
- ½ cup pumpkin puree
- ½ teaspoon ground cinnamon
- 1 pinch ground cloves
- 1 pinch ground nutmeg
- ½ cup frozen whipped topping, thawed

## Directions

**Step 1**

Preheat oven to 325 degrees F (165 degrees C).

**Step 2**

In a large bowl, combine cream cheese, sugar and vanilla. Beat until smooth. Blend in eggs one at a time. Remove 1 cup of batter and spread into bottom of crust; set aside.

**Step 3**

Add pumpkin, cinnamon, cloves and nutmeg to the remaining batter and stir gently until well blended. Carefully spread over the batter in the crust.

**Step 4**

Bake in preheated oven for 35 to 40 minutes, or until center is almost set. Allow to cool, then refrigerate for 3 hours or overnight. Cover with whipped topping before serving.

**Nutrition Facts**

**Per Serving:**

426.3 calories; protein 7.2g 14% DV; carbohydrates 35.5g 12% DV; fat 29g 45% DV; cholesterol 108.1mg 36% DV; sodium 354.4mg 14% DV.

# Too Much Chocolate Cake

**Servings:** 12 **Yield:** 1 12 cup Bundt cake

## Ingredients

- 1 (18.25 ounce) package devil's food cake mix
- 1 (5.9 ounce) package instant chocolate pudding mix
- 1 cup sour cream
- 1 cup vegetable oil
- 4 large eggs eggs
- ½ cup warm water
- 2 cups semisweet chocolate chips

## Directions

### Step 1

Preheat oven to 350 degrees F (175 degrees C).

### Step 2

In a large bowl, mix together the cake and pudding mixes, sour cream, oil, beaten eggs and water. Stir in the chocolate chips and pour batter into a well greased 12 cup bundt pan.

### Step 3

Bake for 50 to 55 minutes, or until top is springy to the touch and a wooden toothpick inserted comes out clean. Cool cake thoroughly in pan at least an hour and a half before inverting onto a plate If desired, dust the cake with powdered sugar.

## Nutrition Facts

**Per Serving:**

600.4 calories; protein 7.6g 15% DV; carbohydrates 60.9g 20% DV; fat 38.6g 59% DV; cholesterol 78.9mg 26% DV; sodium 550.4mg 22% DV.

# Golden Rum Cake

**Prep:** 30 mins **Cook:** 1 hr **Total:** 1 hr 30 mins **Servings:** 12 **Yield:** 1 - 10 inch Bundt pan

## Ingredients

- 1 cup chopped walnuts
- 1 (18.25 ounce) package yellow cake mix

- 1 (3.4 ounce) package instant vanilla pudding mix
- 4 large eggs eggs
- ½ cup water
- ½ cup vegetable oil
- ½ cup dark rum
- ½ cup butter
- ¼ cup water
- 1 cup white sugar
- ½ cup dark rum

## Directions

### Step 1

Preheat oven to 325 degrees F (165 degrees C). Grease and flour a 10 inch Bundt pan. Sprinkle chopped nuts evenly over the bottom of the pan.

### Step 2

In a large bowl, combine cake mix and pudding mix. Mix in the eggs, 1/2 cup water, oil and 1/2 cup rum. Blend well. Pour batter over chopped nuts in the pan.

### Step 3

Bake in the preheated oven for 60 minutes, or until a toothpick inserted into the cake comes out clean. Let sit for 10 minutes in the pan, then turn out onto serving plate. Brush glaze over top and sides. Allow cake to absorb glaze and repeat until all glaze is used.

### Step 4

To make the glaze: in a saucepan, combine butter, 1/4 cup water and 1 cup sugar. Bring to a boil over medium heat and continue to boil for 5 minutes, stirring constantly. Remove from heat and stir in 1/2 cup rum.

## Nutrition Facts

**Per Serving:**

561.8 calories; protein 5.6g 11% DV; carbohydrates 59.2g 19% DV; fat 29.9g 46% DV; cholesterol 83.2mg 28% DV; sodium 476mg 19% DV.

# New York Cheesecake

**Prep:** 30 mins **Cook:** 1 hr **Additional:** 6 hrs **Total:** 7 hrs 30 mins **Servings:** 12 **Yield:** 1 9-inch springform pan

## Ingredients

- 15 large rectangular piece or 2 squares or 4 small rectangular pieces graham crackers, crushed
- 2 tablespoons butter, melted
- 4 (8 ounce) packages cream cheese
- 1 ½ cups white sugar
- ¾ cup milk
- 4 large eggs eggs
- 1 cup sour cream
- 1 tablespoon vanilla extract
- ¼ cup all-purpose flour

**Directions**

**Step 1**

Preheat oven to 350 degrees F (175 degrees C). Grease a 9 inch springform pan.

**Step 2**

In a medium bowl, mix graham cracker crumbs with melted butter. Press onto bottom of springform pan.

**Step 3**

In a large bowl, mix cream cheese with sugar until smooth. Blend in milk, and then mix in the eggs one at a time, mixing just enough to incorporate. Mix in sour cream, vanilla and flour until smooth. Pour filling into prepared crust.

**Step 4**

Bake in preheated oven for 1 hour. Turn the oven off, and let cake cool in oven with the door closed for 5 to 6 hours; this prevents cracking. Chill in refrigerator until serving.

**Nutrition Facts**

**Per Serving:**

533.4 calories; protein 10.3g 21% DV; carbohydrates 44.2g 14% DV; fat 35.7g 55% DV; cholesterol 158.9mg 53% DV; sodium 380.4mg 15% DV.

# Pumpkin Roll

**Prep:** 15 mins **Cook:** 25 mins **Additional:** 20 mins **Total:** 1 hr **Servings:** 10 **Yield:** 10 servings

### Ingredients

- 3 large eggs eggs, beaten
- 1 cup white sugar
- ½ teaspoon ground cinnamon
- ⅔ cup pumpkin puree
- ¾ cup all-purpose flour
- 1 teaspoon baking soda
- 2 tablespoons butter, softened
- 8 ounces cream cheese
- 1 cup confectioners' sugar
- ¼ teaspoon vanilla extract

- confectioners' sugar for dusting

## Directions

### Step 1

Preheat oven to 375 degrees F (190 degrees C). Butter or grease one 10x15 inch jelly roll pan.

### Step 2

In a mixing bowl, blend together the eggs, sugar, cinnamon, and pumpkin. In a separate bowl, mix together flour and baking soda. Add to pumpkin mixture and blend until smooth. Evenly spread the mixture over the prepared jelly roll pan.

### Step 3

Bake 15 to 25 minutes in the preheated oven. Remove from oven and allow to cool enough to handle.

### Step 4

Remove cake from pan and place on tea towel (cotton, not terry cloth). Roll up the cake by rolling a towel inside cake and place seam side down to cool.

### Step 5

Prepare the frosting by blending together the butter, cream cheese, confectioners sugar, and vanilla.

### Step 6

When cake is completely cooled, unroll and spread with cream cheese filling. Roll up again without towel. Wrap with plastic wrap and refrigerate until ready to serve. Sprinkle top with confectioners sugar and slice into 8-10 servings.

### Nutrition Facts

### Per Serving:

288.8 calories; protein 4.7g 9% DV; carbohydrates 42.2g 14% DV; fat 11.8g 18% DV; cholesterol 86.9mg 29% DV; sodium 230.9mg 9% DV.

# Pecan Sour Cream Coffee Cake

**Prep:** 25 mins **Cook:** 30 mins **Total:** 55 mins **Servings:** 8 **Yield:** 8 servings

## Ingredients

### Crumb:

- 1 ½ cups pecans, finely chopped
- ⅓ cup white sugar
- ⅓ cup packed light brown sugar
- 1 teaspoon cinnamon
- ⅛ teaspoon salt
- 3 tablespoons melted butter

## Cake:

- 1 ⅞ cups all-purpose flour
- ½ teaspoon fine sea salt
- 1 teaspoon baking powder
- ¾ teaspoon baking soda
- ½ cup butter
- 1 cup white sugar
- 2 large eggs large eggs
- 1 ½ teaspoons vanilla extract
- 1 cup sour cream or creme fraiche

**Directions**

**Step 1**

Preheat oven to 350 degrees F (175 degrees C). Butter an 8-inch by 10-inch baking dish.

**Step 2**

Mix pecans, 1/3 cup white sugar, brown sugar, cinnamon, salt, and melted butter thoroughly in a mixing bowl until all components are coated with butter, 3 to 4 minutes.

**Step 3**

In a separate bowl, whisk together flour, salt, baking powder, and baking soda.

**Step 4**

In another bowl, mix together butter and 1 cup sugar with a spatula until well blended. Add 1 egg and whisk until mixture is smooth, 2 to 3 minutes. Whisk in second egg until thoroughly incorporated. Add vanilla and sour cream; whisk together. Add flour mixture to wet ingredients; whisk until flour disappears (do not over mix).

**Step 5**

Spread one half of the batter evenly into the bottom of the prepared baking dish. Scatter one half of the crumb mixture evenly over the top of the batter. Top with the rest of the batter and spread carefully to evenly distribute, trying not to disturb the crumbs. Top with the rest of the crumb mixture. Very gently press crumbs into batter. Bake in preheated oven until a bamboo skewer comes out clean, 30 to 35 minutes. Let cool slightly before serving.

**Cook's Note:**

When measuring flour, it's best to gently spoon the flour into your measuring cup. If you dip the cup into the flour it packs the flour and you'll end up with more flour than is called for.

**Nutrition Facts**

# Italian Cream Cheese and Ricotta Cheesecake

**Prep:** 15 mins **Cook:** 2 hrs **Additional:** 4 hrs **Total:** 6 hrs 15 mins **Servings:** 8 **Yield:** 1 9-inch cheesecake

## Ingredients

- 2 (8 ounce) packages cream cheese, softened
- 1 (16 ounce) container ricotta cheese
- 1 ½ cups white sugar
- 4 large eggs eggs
- 1 tablespoon lemon juice
- 1 teaspoon vanilla extract
- 3 tablespoons cornstarch
- 3 tablespoons flour
- ½ cup butter, melted and cooled
- 1 pint sour cream

## Directions

### Step 1

Preheat oven to 350 degrees F (175 degrees C). Lightly grease a 9-inch springform pan.

### Step 2

Mix the cream cheese and ricotta cheese together in a mixing bowl until well combined. Stir in the sugar, eggs, lemon juice, vanilla, cornstarch, flour, and butter. Add the sour cream last and stir. Pour the mixture into the prepared springform pan.

### Step 3

Bake in the preheated oven 1 hour; turn oven off and leave in oven 1 hour more. Allow to cool completely in refrigerator before serving.

**Nutrition Facts**

**Per Serving:**

703.5 calories; protein 16.1g 32% DV; carbohydrates 49.8g 16% DV; fat 50.1g 77% DV; cholesterol 228mg 76% DV; sodium 384.2mg 15% DV.

# Incredibly Delicious Italian Cream Cake

**Prep:** 30 mins **Cook:** 35 mins **Additional:** 30 mins **Total:** 1 hr 35 mins **Servings:** 12 **Yield:** 1 3-layer 9-inch round cake

## Ingredients

- 1 cup buttermilk
- 1 teaspoon baking soda
- ½ cup butter
- ½ cup shortening
- 2 cups white sugar
- 5 large eggs eggs
- 1 teaspoon vanilla extract
- 1 cup flaked coconut
- 1 teaspoon baking powder

- 2 cups all-purpose flour
- 8 ounces cream cheese
- ½ cup butter
- 1 teaspoon vanilla extract
- 4 cups confectioners' sugar
- 2 tablespoons light cream
- ½ cup chopped walnuts
- 1 cup sweetened flaked coconut

## Directions

### Step 1

Preheat oven to 350 degrees F (175 degrees C). Grease three 9 inch round cake pans. In a small bowl, dissolve the baking soda in the buttermilk; set aside.

### Step 2

In a large bowl, cream together 1/2 cup butter, shortening and white sugar until light and fluffy. Mix in the eggs, buttermilk mixture, 1 teaspoon vanilla, 1 cup coconut, baking powder and flour. Stir until just combined. Pour batter into the prepared pans.

### Step 3

Bake in the preheated oven for 30 to 35 minutes, or until a toothpick inserted into the center of the cake comes out clean. Allow to cool.

### Step 4

To Make Frosting: In a medium bowl, combine cream cheese, 1/2 cup butter, 1 teaspoon vanilla and confectioners' sugar. Beat until light and fluffy. Mix in a small amount of cream to attain the desired consistency. Stir in chopped nuts and remaining flaked coconut. Spread between layers and on top and sides of cooled cake.

**Nutrition Facts**

**Per Serving:**

766.7 calories; protein 8.2g 16% DV; carbohydrates 98g 32% DV; fat 39.7g 61% DV; cholesterol 139.8mg 47% DV; sodium 397.2mg 16% DV.

# White Chocolate Raspberry Cheesecake

**Prep:** 1 hr **Cook:** 1 hr **Additional:** 8 hrs **Total:** 10 hrs **Servings:** 16 **Yield:** 1 - 9 inch cheesecake

## Ingredients

- 1 cup chocolate cookie crumbs
- 3 tablespoons white sugar
- ¼ cup butter, melted
- 1 (10 ounce) package frozen raspberries
- 2 tablespoons white sugar
- 2 teaspoons cornstarch
- ½ cup water

- 2 cups white chocolate chips
- ½ cup half-and-half cream
- 3 (8 ounce) packages cream cheese, softened
- ½ cup white sugar
- 3 large eggs eggs
- 1 teaspoon vanilla extract

## Directions

### Step 1

In a medium bowl, mix together cookie crumbs, 3 tablespoons sugar, and melted butter. Press mixture into the bottom of a 9 inch springform pan.

### Step 2

In a saucepan, combine raspberries, 2 tablespoons sugar, cornstarch, and water. Bring to boil, and continue boiling 5 minutes, or until sauce is thick. Strain sauce through a mesh strainer to remove seeds.

### Step 3

Preheat oven to 325 degrees F (165 degrees C). In a metal bowl over a pan of simmering water, melt white chocolate chips with half-and-half, stirring occasionally until smooth.

### Step 4

In a large bowl, mix together cream cheese and 1/2 cup sugar until smooth. Beat in eggs one at a time. Blend in vanilla and melted white chocolate. Pour half of batter over crust. Spoon 3 tablespoons raspberry sauce over batter. Pour remaining cheesecake batter into pan, and again spoon 3 tablespoons raspberry sauce over the top. Swirl batter with the tip of a knife to create a marbled effect.

### Step 5

Bake for 55 to 60 minutes, or until filling is set. Cool, cover with plastic wrap, and refrigerate for 8 hours before removing from pan. Serve with remaining raspberry sauce.

## Nutrition Facts

412 calories; protein 6.8g 14% DV; carbohydrates 34.4g 11% DV; fat 28.3g 44% DV; cholesterol 96.4mg 32% DV; sodium 225.8mg 9% DV.

# Carrot Cake

**Prep:** 30 mins **Cook:** 55 mins **Additional:** 35 mins **Total:** 2 hrs **Servings:** 15 **Yield:** 15 to 18 servings

## Ingredients

- 2 cups white sugar
- ¾ cup vegetable oil
- 3 large eggs eggs
- 1 teaspoon vanilla extract
- ¾ cup buttermilk
- 2 cups grated carrots
- 1 cup flaked coconut
- 1 (15 ounce) can crushed pineapple, drained
- 2 cups all-purpose flour

- 2 teaspoons baking soda
- 2 teaspoons ground cinnamon
- 1 ½ teaspoons salt
- 1 cup chopped walnuts
- ½ cup butter
- 1 (8 ounce) package cream cheese
- 1 teaspoon vanilla extract
- 4 cups confectioners' sugar

## Directions

### Step 1

Preheat oven to 350 degrees F (175 degrees C). Grease a 9x13 inch baking pan. Set aside.

### Step 2

In a large bowl, mix together sugar, oil, eggs, vanilla, and buttermilk. Stir in carrots, coconut, vanilla, and pineapple. In a separate bowl, combine flour, baking soda, cinnamon, and salt; gently stir into carrot mixture. Stir in chopped nuts. Spread batter into prepared pan.

### Step 3

Bake for 55 minutes or until toothpick inserted into cake comes out clean. Remove from oven, and set aside to cool.

### Step 4

In a medium mixing bowl, combine butter or margarine, cream cheese, vanilla, and confectioners sugar. Blend until creamy. Frost cake while still in the pan.

**Nutrition Facts**

**Per Serving:**

615.5 calories; protein 6.2g 12% DV; carbohydrates 83.5g 27% DV; fat 30.2g 46% DV; cholesterol 70.4mg 24% DV; sodium 540.4mg 22% DV.

# Make-Ahead Sour Cream Coffee Cake

**Prep:** 15 mins **Cook:** 35 mins **Additional:** 8 hrs **Total:** 8 hrs 50 mins **Servings:** 15 **Yield:** 1 9x13-inch coffee cake

## Ingredients

- ¾ cup butter, softened
- 1 cup white sugar
- 2 large eggs eggs
- 1 (8 ounce) carton sour cream
- 2 cups all-purpose flour
- 1 teaspoon baking powder

- 1 teaspoon baking soda
- 1 teaspoon ground nutmeg
- ½ teaspoon salt
- ¾ cup packed brown sugar
- ½ cup chopped pecans
- 1 teaspoon ground cinnamon

## Directions

### Step 1

Grease and flour a 9x13-inch baking pan.

### Step 2

Beat butter and white sugar in a bowl with an electric mixer until light and fluffy, about 2 minutes.

### Step 3

Beat eggs and sour cream into butter mixture until smooth.

### Step 4

Whisk flour, baking powder, baking soda, nutmeg, and salt together in a bowl until thoroughly combined; stir into the sour cream mixture to make a batter.

### Step 5

Pour the batter into the prepared baking dish.

### Step 6

Mix the brown sugar, pecans, and cinnamon in a bowl; sprinkle the mixture over the batter.

### Step 7

Cover the baking dish with plastic wrap and chill 8 hours to overnight.

**Step 8**

Preheat oven to 350 degrees F (175 degrees C).

**Step 9**

Remove plastic wrap from the dish; bake until a toothpick inserted into the center of the coffee cake comes out clean, 35 to 40 minutes.

**Nutrition Facts**

**Per Serving:**

304 calories; protein 3.5g 7% DV; carbohydrates 38.3g 12% DV; fat 15.9g 25% DV; cholesterol 55.9mg 19% DV; sodium 271.6mg 11% DV.

# Ricotta Pie (Old Italian Recipe)

**Prep:** 45 mins **Cook:** 45 mins **Additional:** 1 hr 30 mins **Total:** 3 hrs **Servings:** 24 **Yield:** 2 deep-dish pies

**Ingredients**

**Pie Filling:**

- 12 large eggs eggs
- 2 cups white sugar
- 2 teaspoons vanilla extract

- 3 pounds ricotta cheese
- ¼ cup miniature semisweet chocolate chips, or to taste

**Sweet Crust:**

- 4 cups all-purpose flour
- 5 teaspoons baking powder
- 1 cup white sugar
- ½ cup shortening, chilled

- 1 tablespoon shortening, chilled
- 4 large eggs eggs, lightly beaten
- 1 teaspoon vanilla extract
- 1 tablespoon milk

**Directions**

**Step 1**

Beat the 12 eggs, 2 cups sugar and vanilla extract together in a large bowl. Stir in the ricotta cheese and the chocolate chips, if using (see Cook's Note). Set aside.

**Step 2**

Combine the flour, baking powder, and 1 cup sugar together. Cut in 1/2 cup plus 1 tablespoon shortening until the mixture resembles coarse crumbs. Mix in 4 beaten eggs and 1 teaspoon vanilla extract. Divide dough into 4 balls, wrap in plastic, and chill for at least 30 minutes.

## Step 3

Preheat oven to 325 degrees F (165 degrees C). Grease two deep-dish pie plates.

## Step 4

Roll out 2 of the balls to fit into the pie pans. Do not make the crust too thick, as it will expand during cooking. Do not flute the edges of the dough. Roll out the other 2 balls of dough and cut each into 8 narrow strips for the top of the crust. (Alternately, you can use cookie cutters and place the cutouts on the top of the pies.)

## Step 5

Pour the ricotta filling evenly into the pie crusts. Top each pie with 8 narrow strips of dough or cookie cut-outs. Brush top of pie with milk for shine, if desired. Place foil on the edge of crust.

## Step 6

Bake in preheated oven for 20 to 30 minutes; remove foil. Rotate pies on the rack so they will bake evenly. Continue to bake until a knife inserted in the center of each pie comes out clean, 25 to 30 minutes more. Cool completely on wire racks. Refrigerate until serving.

**Nutrition Facts**

**Per Serving:**

352.1 calories; protein 12.9g 26% DV; carbohydrates 45.6g 15% DV; fat 13.4g 21% DV; cholesterol 141.6mg 47% DV; sodium 220.1mg 9% DV.

# Pumpkin Roll

**Prep:** 20 mins **Cook:** 15 mins **Additional:** 20 mins **Total:** 55 mins **Servings:** 10 **Yield:** 10 servings

## Ingredients

- ¾ cup all-purpose flour
- 1 cup white sugar
- 1 teaspoon baking soda
- 2 teaspoons pumpkin pie spice
- 1 cup pumpkin puree
- 3 large eggs eggs

- 1 teaspoon lemon juice
- 2 tablespoons confectioners' sugar
- 1 (8 ounce) package cream cheese, softened
- ¼ cup butter
- 1 teaspoon vanilla extract
- 1 cup confectioners' sugar

**Directions**

**Step 1**

Preheat oven to 375 degrees F (190 degrees C). Grease and flour a 9x13 inch jelly roll pan or cookie sheet.

**Step 2**

In a large bowl, mix together flour, sugar, baking soda, and pumpkin pie spice. Stir in pumpkin puree, eggs, and lemon juice. Pour mixture into prepared pan. Spread the mixture evenly.

**Step 3**

Bake at 375 degrees F (190 degrees C) for 15 minutes.

**Step 4**

Lay a damp linen towel on the counter, sprinkle it with confectioner's sugar, and turn the cake onto the towel. Carefully roll the towel up (lengthwise) with the cake in it. Place the cake-in-towel on a cooling rack and let it cool for 20 minutes.

**Step 5**

Make the icing: In a medium bowl, blend cream cheese, butter, vanilla, and sugar with a wooden spoon or electric mixer.

**Step 6**

When the cake has cooled 20 minutes, unroll it and spread icing onto it. Immediately re-roll (not in the towel this time), and wrap it with plastic wrap. Keep the cake refrigerated or freeze it for up to 2 weeks in aluminum foil. Cut the cake in slices just before serving.

**Nutrition Facts**

**Per Serving:**

315.6 calories; protein 4.9g 10% DV; carbohydrates 43.7g 14% DV; fat 14.1g 22% DV; cholesterol 92.6mg 31% DV; sodium 305.5mg 12% DV.

# Best Boiled Fruitcake

**Servings:** 10 **Yield:** 1 - 8 inch cake

## Ingredients

- 12 ounces candied mixed fruit
- 5 ounces glace cherries, roughly chopped
- 2 ounces candied mixed citrus peel
- 2 ounces chopped walnuts
- ¾ cup butter
- 1 teaspoon ground allspice
- ½ teaspoon baking soda
- 1 cup milk
- 12 ounces sifted self-rising flour
- 2 large eggs eggs
- 1 ½ cups white sugar

## Directions

### Step 1

Preheat oven to 325 degrees F (160 degrees C). Line one 8 inch deep sided cake tin with parchment paper.

### Step 2

Place the fruit cherries, peel, walnuts, sugar, butter or margarine, mixed spice, baking soda and milk in a medium sized saucepan. Bring to a boil and simmer for 5 minutes. Let mixture cool to body temperature.

### Step 3

Stir in the flour and the eggs. Pour batter into the prepared pan. Wrap outside of pan with brown paper or newspaper.

### Step 4

Bake at 325 degrees F (160 degrees C) for 40 minutes then reduce temperature to 300 degrees F (150 degrees C) and continue to baking cake for 1-1/2 hours. Remove cake from oven and allow it to cool in tin for 5 minutes then turn it out onto a cooling rack, remove greaseproof paper and leave until cool. Cake can be stored for up to 6 months wrapped in foil and in an air tight tin.

## Nutrition Facts

### Per Serving:

587.5 calories; protein 6.6g 13% DV; carbohydrates 99.4g 32% DV; fat 19.4g 30% DV; cholesterol 75.8mg 25% DV; sodium 621.1mg 25% DV.

# Tiramisu Cheesecake

**Prep:** 30 mins **Cook:** 40 mins **Additional:** 3 hrs 50 mins **Total:** 5 hrs **Servings:** 12 **Yield:** 1 8-inch cheesecake

## Ingredients

- 1 (12 ounce) package ladyfingers
- ¼ cup butter, melted
- ¼ cup coffee-flavored liqueur, divided
- 3 (8 ounce) packages cream cheese
- 1 (8 ounce) container mascarpone cheese
- 1 cup white sugar
- 2 large eggs eggs
- ¼ cup all-purpose flour
- 1 (1 ounce) square semisweet chocolate

## Directions

### Step 1

Preheat oven to 350 degrees F (175 degrees C). Place a pan of water on the bottom of the oven.

### Step 2

Crush the package of ladyfingers to fine crumbs. Mix the melted butter into the crumbs. Moisten with 2 tablespoons of the coffee liqueur. Press into an 8-inch springform pan.

### Step 3

In a large bowl, mix cream cheese, mascarpone, and sugar until very smooth. Add 2 tablespoons coffee liqueur, and mix. Add the eggs and the flour; mix slowly just until smooth. Pour batter over crust in the springform pan.

### Step 4

Place pan on middle rack of oven. Bake until just set, 40 to 45 minutes. Open oven door, and turn off the heat. Leave cake to cool in oven for 20 minutes. Remove from oven, and let it finish cooling, about 30 minutes. Refrigerate for at least 3 hours, or overnight.

### Step 5

Grate semisweet chocolate over the top right before serving.

### Nutrition Facts

### Per Serving:

528 calories; protein 10.1g 20% DV; carbohydrates 40.2g 13% DV; fat 36.2g 56% DV; cholesterol 188mg 63% DV; sodium 256.4mg 10% DV.

# Pumpkin Dessert

**Prep:** 10 mins **Cook:** 50 mins **Total:** 1 hr **Servings:** 18 **Yield:** 1 9x13 inch baking dish

## Ingredients

- 1 (18.25 ounce) package yellow cake mix
- ⅓ cup butter, melted
- 1 egg
- 1 (29 ounce) can pumpkin
- ½ cup brown sugar
- .66 cup milk
- 3 large eggs eggs
- 2 tablespoons pumpkin pie spice
- ¼ cup butter, chilled
- ½ cup white sugar
- ¾ cup chopped walnuts

## Directions

### Step 1

Preheat oven to 350 degrees F (175 degrees C) and lightly grease a 9x13 inch baking dish.

### Step 2

Set aside 1 cup of cake mix. Combine remaining cake mix with melted butter and 1 egg and mix until well blended; spread mixture in the bottom of the prepared baking dish.

### Step 3

In a large bowl combine pumpkin, brown sugar, milk, 3 eggs and pumpkin pie spice; mix well and pour this mixture over cake mix mixture in baking dish.

### Step 4

In a small bowl with a pastry blender, or in a food processor, combine chilled butter and white sugar with reserved cake mix until mixture resembles coarse crumbs. Sprinkle over pumpkin mixture. Sprinkle chopped walnuts over all.

### Step 5

Bake 45 to 50 minutes, until top is golden.

## Nutrition Facts

### Per Serving:

291.8 calories; protein 4.6g 9% DV; carbohydrates 39.1g 13% DV; fat 14.1g 22% DV; cholesterol 58.3mg 19% DV; sodium 254.1mg 10% DV.

# Fruit Cocktail Cake

**Servings:** 16 **Yield:** 1 - 9 inch square cake

## Ingredients

- 1 cup all-purpose flour
- 1 cup white sugar
- 1 egg
- 1 teaspoon baking soda

- 1 teaspoon vanilla extract
- 1 (16 ounce) can fruit cocktail
- ½ cup packed brown sugar

## Directions

### Step 1

Preheat oven to 350 degrees F (175 degrees C). Lightly grease one 9x9 inch square baking pan.

### Step 2

Combine the flour, white sugar, egg, baking soda, vanilla and undrained fruit cocktail. Mix until blended. Pour batter into the prepared pan and sprinkle the top with the brown sugar.

### Step 3

Bake at 350 degrees F (175 degrees C) for 40 minutes or until golden brown and firm.

## Nutrition Facts

### Per Serving:

132.8 calories; protein 1.3g 3% DV; carbohydrates 31.7g 10% DV; fat 0.4g 1% DV; cholesterol 11.6mg 4% DV; sodium 86.8mg 4% DV.

# Persimmon Pudding

**Prep:** 20 mins **Cook:** 55 mins **Total:** 1 hr 15 mins **Servings:** 8 **Yield:** 8 servings

## Ingredients

- ½ teaspoon baking soda
- 2 cups persimmon pulp
- 2 ½ cups white sugar
- 2 large eggs eggs, beaten
- 2 cups all-purpose flour
- 2 teaspoons baking powder

- ½ teaspoon ground cinnamon
- ¼ teaspoon vanilla extract
- 1 pinch salt
- 2 ½ cups milk
- 4 tablespoons melted butter

## Directions

## Step 1

Preheat oven to 325 degrees F (165 degrees C). Grease a 9x13-inch baking dish.

## Step 2

In a mixing bowl, combine persimmon pulp, baking soda, sugar and eggs. Mix well.

## Step 3

Add flour, baking powder, cinnamon, vanilla, salt, milk and melted butter. Stir to combine.

## Step 4

Pour into baking pan and bake in preheated oven for 55 minutes. The pudding will rise but will fall when removed from oven.

### Nutrition Facts

### Per Serving:

538.5 calories; protein 7.9g 16% DV; carbohydrates 110.1g 36% DV; fat 9g 14% DV; cholesterol 67.9mg 23% DV; sodium 310.8mg 12% DV.

# Chocolate Lava Cake

**Prep:** 5 mins **Cook:** 25 mins **Additional:** 45 mins **Total:** 1 hr 15 mins **Servings:** 4 **Yield:** 4 servings

### Ingredients

- butter as needed
- 2 large egg yolks egg yolks
- 2 large eggs eggs
- 3 tablespoons white sugar
- 3 ½ ounces chopped dark chocolate
- 5 tablespoons butter
- 4 teaspoons unsweetened cocoa powder
- 3 tablespoons flour
- 1 pinch salt
- ⅛ teaspoon vanilla extract

### Directions

### Step 1

Generously butter the inside of 4 (5 1/2 ounce) ramekins. Place them in a casserole dish.

### Step 2

Whisk together egg yolks, eggs, and sugar in a bowl until light, foamy, and lemon colored.

### Step 3

Melt chocolate and butter in a microwave-safe bowl in 30-second intervals, stirring after each melting, 1 to 3 minutes.

**Step 4**

Stir melted chocolate mixture into egg and sugar mixture until combined.

**Step 5**

Sift cocoa powder into the mixture; stir to combine.

**Step 6**

Sift flour and salt into the mixture; stir to combine into a batter.

**Step 7**

Stir vanilla extract into the batter.

**Step 8**

Transfer batter to a resealable plastic bag. Snip one corner of the bag with scissors to create a tip.

**Step 9**

Divide batter evenly between the prepared ramekins; tap gently on the counter to remove any air bubbles.

**Step 10**

Refrigerate 30 minutes.

**Step 11**

Preheat an oven to 425 degrees F (220 degrees C).

**Step 12**

Arrange the ramekins in a casserole dish. Pour enough hot tap water into the casserole dish to reach halfway up the sides of the ramekins.

**Step 13**

Bake in the preheated over for 15-18 minutes. Set aside to cool for 15 minutes.

**Step 14**

Loosen the edges from the ramekin with a knife. Invert each cake onto a plate and dust with powdered sugar.

Per Serving:

393.7 calories; protein 6.9g 14% DV; carbohydrates 32g 10% DV; fat 28.7g 44% DV; cholesterol 241.2mg 80% DV; sodium 207.4mg 8% DV.

# Cake Balls

**Prep:** 40 mins **Cook:** 30 mins **Additional:** 2 hrs **Total:** 3 hrs 10 mins **Servings:** 36 **Yield:** 3 dozen

## Ingredients

- 1 (18.25 ounce) package chocolate cake mix
- 1 (16 ounce) container prepared chocolate frosting
- 1 (3 ounce) bar chocolate flavored confectioners coating

## Directions

### Step 1

Prepare the cake mix according to package directions using any of the recommended pan sizes. When cake is done, crumble while warm into a large bowl, and stir in the frosting until well blended.

### Step 2

Melt chocolate coating in a glass bowl in the microwave, or in a metal bowl over a pan of simmering water, stirring occasionally until smooth.

### Step 3

Use a melon baller or small scoop to form balls of the chocolate cake mixture. Dip the balls in chocolate using a toothpick or fork to hold them. Place on waxed paper to set.

### Nutrition Facts

### Per Serving:

123.6 calories; protein 1.1g 2% DV; carbohydrates 19.7g 6% DV; fat 5.2g 8% DV; cholesterol 0.5mg; sodium 143.4mg 6% DV.

# Old-Fashioned Persimmon Pudding

**Prep:** 25 mins **Cook:** 1 hr **Additional:** 30 mins **Total:** 1 hr 55 mins **Servings:** 12 **Yield:** 1 9x13-inch dish

## Ingredients

- cooking spray
- 4 cups all-purpose flour
- 1 teaspoon baking soda
- 1 teaspoon baking powder
- ½ teaspoon salt
- 1 teaspoon cinnamon

- 1 cup white sugar
- 1 cup brown sugar
- 3 large eggs eggs, beaten
- 2 cups milk
- 2 ½ cups persimmon pulp
- 6 tablespoons butter, melted

## Directions

### Step 1

Preheat oven to 300 degrees F (150 degrees C). Spray a 9x13-inch baking dish with cooking spray.

### Step 2

In a bowl, whisk together the flour, baking soda, baking powder, salt, cinnamon, white sugar, and brown sugar until thoroughly combined. In a large bowl, beat the eggs and milk together until smooth, and add the flour mixture, alternating with the persimmon pulp in several additions, mixing well after each addition. Stir in the melted butter. Scrape the batter into the prepared baking dish.

### Step 3

Bake in the preheated oven until a toothpick inserted into the pudding comes out clean, about 1 hour. Allow to cool before serving.

### Nutrition Facts

### Per Serving:

438 calories; protein 7.7g 15% DV; carbohydrates 85.1g 28% DV; fat 8.4g 13% DV; cholesterol 65mg 22% DV; sodium 324mg 13% DV.

# Buche de Noel

**Prep:** 45 mins **Cook:** 15 mins **Additional:** 30 mins **Total:** 1 hr 30 mins **Servings:** 12 **Yield:** 1 buche de Noel

## Ingredients

- 2 cups heavy cream
- ½ cup confectioners' sugar
- ½ cup unsweetened cocoa powder
- 1 teaspoon vanilla extract
- 6 large egg yolks egg yolks
- ½ cup white sugar
- ⅓ cup unsweetened cocoa powder
- 1 ½ teaspoons vanilla extract
- ⅛ teaspoon salt
- 6 large egg whites egg whites
- ¼ cup white sugar
- confectioners' sugar for dusting

## Directions

### Step 1

Preheat oven to 375 degrees F (190 degrees C). Line a 10x15 inch jellyroll pan with parchment paper. In a large bowl, whip cream, 1/2 cup confectioners' sugar, 1/2 cup cocoa, and 1 teaspoon vanilla until thick and stiff. Refrigerate.

### Step 2

In a large bowl, use an electric mixer to beat egg yolks with 1/2 cup sugar until thick and pale. Blend in 1/3 cup cocoa, 1 1/2 teaspoons vanilla, and salt. In large glass bowl, using clean beaters, whip egg whites to soft peaks. Gradually add 1/4 cup sugar, and beat until whites form stiff peaks. Immediately fold the yolk mixture into the whites. Spread the batter evenly into the prepared pan.

### Step 3

Bake for 12 to 15 minutes in the preheated oven, or until the cake springs back when lightly touched. Dust a clean dishtowel with confectioners' sugar. Run a knife around the edge of the pan, and turn the warm cake out onto the towel. Remove and discard parchment paper. Starting at the short edge of the cake, roll the cake up with the towel. Cool for 30 minutes.

### Step 4

Unroll the cake, and spread the filling to within 1 inch of the edge. Roll the cake up with the filling inside. Place seam side down onto a serving plate, and refrigerate until serving. Dust with confectioners' sugar before serving.

**Nutrition Facts**

**Per Serving:**

275.6 calories; protein 5.1g 10% DV; carbohydrates 27.6g 9% DV; fat 17.7g 27% DV; cholesterol 156.8mg 52% DV; sodium 72.4mg 3% DV.

# Jamaican Fruit Cake

**Prep:** 20 mins **Cook:** 1 hr 30 mins **Total:** 1 hr 50 mins **Servings:** 12 **Yield:** 2 - 9 inch round cake pans

## Ingredients

- 2 cups butter
- 2 cups white sugar
- 9 large eggs eggs
- ¼ cup white rum
- 1 tablespoon lime juice
- 1 teaspoon vanilla extract
- 1 tablespoon almond extract
- 1 grated zest of one lime
- 2 pounds chopped dried mixed fruit

- 2 cups red wine
- 1 cup dark molasses
- 2 ½ cups all-purpose flour
- 3 teaspoons baking powder
- ½ teaspoon ground nutmeg
- ½ teaspoon ground allspice
- ½ teaspoon ground cinnamon
- 1 pinch salt

## Directions

### Step 1

Preheat oven to 350 degrees F (175 degrees C). Grease and flour 2 - 9 inch round cake pans.

### Step 2

In a large bowl, cream together the butter and sugar until light and fluffy. Beat in eggs, then add rum, lime juice, vanilla, almond extract, and lime zest. Stir in mixed fruit, wine, and molasses. Sift together flour, baking powder, nutmeg, allspice, cinnamon, and salt. Fold into batter, being careful not to over-mix. Pour into prepared pans.

### Step 3

Bake in preheated oven for 80 to 90 minutes, or until a knife inserted into the center comes out clean. Let cool in pan for 10 minutes, then turn out onto a wire rack and cool completely.

## Nutrition Facts

### Per Serving:

862 calories; protein 9.6g 19% DV; carbohydrates 124.2g 40% DV; fat 35.1g 54% DV; cholesterol 220.8mg 74% DV; sodium 418.4mg 17% DV.

# Irish Cream Bundt Cake

**Prep:** 15 mins **Cook:** 1 hr **Additional:** 15 mins **Total:** 1 hr 30 mins **Servings:** 12 **Yield:** 1 - 10 inch Bundt pan

## Ingredients

- 1 cup chopped pecans
- 1 (18.25 ounce) package yellow cake mix
- 1 (3.4 ounce) package instant vanilla pudding mix
- 4 large eggs eggs
- ¼ cup water

- ½ cup vegetable oil
- ¾ cup Irish cream liqueur
- ½ cup butter
- ¼ cup water
- 1 cup white sugar
- ¼ cup Irish cream liqueur

## Directions

### Step 1

Preheat oven to 325 degrees F (165 degrees C). Grease and flour a 10 inch Bundt pan. Sprinkle chopped nuts evenly over bottom of pan.

### Step 2

In a large bowl, combine cake mix and pudding mix. Mix in eggs, 1/4 cup water, 1/2 cup oil and 3/4 cup Irish cream liqueur. Beat for 5 minutes at high speed. Pour batter over nuts in pan.

### Step 3

Bake in the preheated oven for 60 minutes, or until a toothpick inserted into the cake comes out clean. Cool for 10 minutes in the pan, then invert onto the serving dish. Prick top and sides of cake. Spoon glaze over top and brush onto sides of cake. Allow to absorb glaze repeat until all glaze is used up.

### Step 4

To make the glaze: In a saucepan, combine butter, 1/4 cup water and 1 cup sugar. Bring to a boil and continue boiling for 5 minutes, stirring constantly. Remove from heat and stir in 1/4 cup Irish cream.

## Nutrition Facts

### Per Serving:

590.2 calories; protein 4.9g 10% DV; carbohydrates 68.4g 22% DV; fat 30.1g 46% DV; cholesterol 83.2mg 28% DV; sodium 476.6mg 19% DV.

# Creamy Coconut Cake

**Prep:** 20 mins **Cook:** 35 mins **Additional:** 1 hr 30 mins **Total:** 2 hrs 25 mins **Servings:** 12 **Yield:** 12 servings

## Ingredients

- 1 (16 ounce) package white cake mix
- 1 (14 ounce) can cream of coconut
- 1 (14 ounce) can sweetened condensed milk
- 1 (16 ounce) container frozen whipped topping, thawed
- 1 (10 ounce) package flaked coconut

## Directions

### Step 1

Prepare cake according to package directions. Bake in a 9x13 inch pan. Cool completely.

### Step 2

In a small bowl combine cream of coconut and condensed milk.

### Step 3

Poke holes in cake with a straw. Pour milk mixture over cake and spread with whipped topping. Sprinkle coconut over cake.

### Step 4

Serve chilled.

## Nutrition Facts

### Per Serving:

605.6 calories; protein 5.8g 12% DV; carbohydrates 85g 27% DV; fat 28.2g 43% DV; cholesterol 11.1mg 4% DV; sodium 377mg 15% DV.

# Figgy Pudding

**Prep:** 15 mins **Cook:** 2 hrs 10 mins **Additional:** 10 mins **Total:** 2 hrs 35 mins **Servings:** 10 **Yield:** 1 tube pan

## Ingredients

- 1 ¾ cups buttermilk
- 12 ounces dried Calimyrna figs, coarsely chopped
- 1 ½ cups white whole-wheat flour (such as King Arthur)
- 1 cup white sugar

- 2 ½ teaspoons baking powder
- 1 teaspoon ground nutmeg
- 1 teaspoon ground cinnamon
- 1 teaspoon salt
- 3 eaches eggs
- 1 ½ cups dry bread crumbs
- ½ cup butter, melted
- 1 (2.45 ounce) package sliced almonds
- 3 tablespoons orange marmalade
- 1 tablespoon grated orange zest
- ½ teaspoon orange-vanilla flavoring (such as Fiori di Sicilia

**Directions**

**Step 1**

Gently heat buttermilk and figs in a saucepan over medium-low heat until softened, 10 to 15 minutes; set aside until cool.

**Step 2**

Preheat oven to 350 degrees F (175 degrees C). Grease a tube pan.

**Step 3**

Sift flour, sugar, baking powder, nutmeg, cinnamon, and salt together in a bowl.

**Step 4**

Beat eggs in a large bowl with an electric hand mixer on high for 1 minute. Add fig-and-buttermilk mixture, bread crumbs, butter, almonds, orange marmalade, orange zest, and orange-vanilla flavoring to the beaten eggs; beat on low speed until blended. Gradually add flour mixture while beating until just incorporated into a batter. Spoon batter into prepared pan. Grease a sheet of aluminum foil; use to cover pan.

**Step 5**

Bake in preheated oven until firm and pulling away from sides of the pan, about 2 hours. Set aside to cool for 10 minutes before removing from pan.

**Nutrition Facts**

**Per Serving:**

465.1 calories; protein 10.4g 21% DV; carbohydrates 75.3g 24% DV; fat 16.1g 25% DV; cholesterol 75.2mg 25% DV; sodium 610.1mg 24% DV.

# Pumpkin Swirled Cheese Cake

**Prep:** 20 mins **Cook:** 52 mins **Total:** 1 hr 12 mins **Servings:** 8 **Yield:** 1 - 9 inch pie

## Ingredients

- 1 ½ cups crushed shortbread cookies
- 3 tablespoons melted butter
- 3 tablespoons unbleached all-purpose flour
- ¾ cup white sugar
- ¼ cup brown sugar
- 3 tablespoons unbleached all-purpose flour
- 1 (8 ounce) package cream cheese, softened
- 1 (3 ounce) package cream cheese, softened

- 1 tablespoon vanilla extract
- 1 teaspoon ground cinnamon
- ¼ teaspoon ground nutmeg
- ¼ teaspoon ground ginger
- 3 large eggs eggs
- 1 (15 ounce) can pumpkin puree
- 1 tablespoon milk

## Directions

### Step 1

Preheat oven to 375 degrees F (190 degrees C.)

### Step 2

In a medium bowl, mix crushed cookies, 3 tablespoons melted butter and 3 tablespoons flour. Press firmly on bottom and side of ungreased 9 inch pie plate. Bake about 12 minutes or until light brown. Allow to cool.

### Step 3

In a large bowl, combine white sugar, brown sugar, flour, and cream cheese. Beat on low speed until smooth. Reserve 1/2 cup of this mixture to swirl in later. To the mixture in the bowl, add vanilla, cinnamon, nutmeg, ginger. Blend in eggs and pumpkin puree. Scrape bowl, and beat until smooth. Pour into crust.

### Step 4

Stir 1 tablespoon milk into the reserved cream cheese mixture. Drop by spoonfuls over the pumpkin mixture. Use a knife to decoratively swirl the two mixtures together.

### Step 5

Cover edge of crust with 2 to 3 inch strip of aluminum foil to prevent excessive browning. Bake in preheated 35 to 40 minutes or until knife inserted in center comes out clean. Remove foil the last 15 minutes of baking. Cool 30 minutes, then refrigerate at least 4 hours before serving.

## Nutrition Facts

# Tennessee Jam Cake

**Prep:** 25 mins **Cook:** 40 mins **Total:** 1 hr 5 mins **Servings:** 12 **Yield:** 1 - 3 layer cake

## Ingredients

- 1 cup butter, softened
- 2 cups white sugar
- 8 large eggs eggs
- 2 teaspoons baking soda
- 2 tablespoons water
- 2 cups seedless blackberry jam
- 3 ½ cups all-purpose flour
- 1 ½ teaspoons ground cloves
- 2 teaspoons ground nutmeg
- 1 tablespoon ground cinnamon
- 1 teaspoon salt
- 1 cup buttermilk
- 1 cup chopped black walnuts
- ½ cup golden raisins

## Directions

### Step 1

Preheat the oven to 350 degrees F (175 degrees C). Grease three 8 or 9 inch round cake pans and set aside.

### Step 2

In a large bowl, beat butter and sugar until light and fluffy. Add eggs one at a time, mixing until each one is blended in. Dissolve the baking soda in the water; stir into the batter along with the blackberry jam. Combine the flour, cloves, nutmeg, cinnamon and salt; stir into the batter by hand, alternating with the buttermilk. Fold in the black walnuts and raisins if using. Divide the batter equally between the three pans, and spread in an even layer.

### Step 3

Bake in the preheated oven until the top of the cakes spring back when lightly touched, about 35 minutes. Cool in the pans until cool enough to handle, then invert the cakes over a wire rack and remove pans to cool completely.

## Nutrition Facts

## Per Serving:

684.9 calories; protein 11.6g 23% DV; carbohydrates 106.6g 34% DV; fat 25.6g 39% DV; cholesterol 165.5mg 55% DV; sodium 583.2mg 23% DV.

# Ultimate Cranberry Pudding Cake

**Prep:** 30 mins **Cook:** 1 hr **Total:** 1 hr 30 mins **Servings:** 12 **Yield:** 1 - 10 inch Bundt pan

## Ingredients

- 6 tablespoons butter
- 2 cups white sugar
- 4 cups all-purpose flour
- 4 teaspoons baking powder
- 1 teaspoon salt
- 2 cups evaporated milk

- 1 (12 ounce) package cranberries
- 1 cup butter
- 2 cups white sugar
- 1 cup heavy cream
- 1 teaspoon vanilla extract

## Directions

### Step 1

Preheat oven to 325 degrees F (165 degrees C). Grease and flour a 10 inch Bundt pan. Mix together the flour, baking powder and salt. Set aside.

### Step 2

In a large bowl, cream together the 6 tablespoons butter and 2 cups sugar until light and fluffy. Beat in the flour mixture alternately with the evaporated milk. Stir in the cranberries. Pour batter into prepared pan.

### Step 3

Bake in the preheated oven for 50 to 60 minutes, or until a toothpick inserted into the center of the cake comes out clean. Let cool in pan for 10 minutes, then turn out onto a wire rack and cool completely.

### Step 4

To make the Hot Butter Sauce: In a saucepan, combine 1 cup butter, 2 cups sugar, and cream. Bring to a boil over medium heat, reduce heat and let simmer for 10 minutes. Remove from heat and stir in vanilla. Serve slices of cake generously covered with hot butter sauce.

## Nutrition Facts

### Per Serving:

735.4 calories; protein 7.9g 16% DV; carbohydrates 107g 35% DV; fat 32.1g 49% DV; cholesterol 95.3mg 32% DV; sodium 517mg 21% DV.

# Irish Cream Cheesecake

**Servings:** 12 **Yield:** 9 inch cheesecake

## Ingredients

- 1 cup graham cracker crumbs
- 3 tablespoons white sugar
- 3 tablespoons melted butter
- 3 (8 ounce) packages cream cheese
- 1 cup white sugar
- 2 teaspoons vanilla extract

- 1 cup sour cream
- ⅓ cup Irish cream liqueur
- 4 large eggs eggs
- 1 cup sour cream
- ¼ cup white sugar

## Directions

### Step 1

Mix together cracker crumbs, 3 tablespoons sugar, and melted butter. Press this crumb mixture into bottom of 9 inch springform pan with 2 3/4 inch high sides. Bake at 350 degrees F (175 degrees) until brown - about 8 minutes. Transfer crust to rack and cool. Maintain oven temperature.

### Step 2

Using electric mixer, beat cream cheese, 1 cup sugar and vanilla in large bowl until blended. Beat in 1 cup sour cream and liqueur. Add eggs one at a time, beating just until combined. Pour filling over crust in pan. Bake until edges are puffed, and center no longer moves when pan is shaken, about 1 to 1/2 hours. Transfer cheesecake to rack, and cool 10 minutes. Maintain oven temperature.

### Step 3

Mix 1 cup sour cream and 1/4 cup sugar in a small bowl until smooth. Press down edges of cheesecake, and spread mixture on top. Bake 10 minutes. Transfer cheesecake to rack and cool. Cover and refrigerate overnight. Release pan from cheesecake. Cut and serve.

## Nutrition Facts

### Per Serving:

476.1 calories; protein 8g 16% DV; carbohydrates 35.8g 12% DV; fat 32.8g 51% DV; cholesterol 148.1mg 49% DV; sodium 272.7mg 11% DV.

# Maritime War Cake

**Prep:** 10 mins **Cook:** 1 hr 10 mins **Additional:** 30 mins **Total:** 1 hr 50 mins **Servings:** 24 **Yield:** 24 servings

## Ingredients

- 2 cups water
- 2 cups raisins
- 1 cup light molasses
- 1 cup white sugar
- ⅔ cup shortening
- 3 cups all-purpose flour
- 1 teaspoon baking soda
- 1 tablespoon ground cinnamon

## Directions

### Step 1

Preheat oven to 325 degrees F (165 degrees C). Grease and flour a round tube pan or two loaf pans.

### Step 2

Bring water, raisins, molasses, sugar, and shortening to a boil in a saucepan; reduce heat to low and simmer until raisins are plump, about 5 minutes. Allow to cool.

### Step 3

Whisk flour, baking soda, and cinnamon together in a bowl. Stir flour mixture into raisin mixture until well combined; pour into prepared baking pan.

### Step 4

Bake in the preheated oven until a toothpick inserted near the center comes out clean, about 1 hour.

**Nutrition Facts**

**Per Serving:**

220.9 calories; protein 2g 4% DV; carbohydrates 41.6g 13% DV; fat 5.9g 9% DV; cholesterolmg; sodium 59.9mg 2% DV.

# Plum Bread

**Prep:** 20 mins **Cook:** 50 mins **Additional:** 10 mins **Total:** 1 hr 20 mins **Servings:** 16 **Yield:** 1 bundt cake

## Ingredients

- 1 cup vegetable oil
- 3 large eggs eggs

- 2 (4 ounce) jars plum baby food
- 2 cups white sugar
- 1 teaspoon red food coloring
- 2 cups all-purpose flour
- 1 teaspoon ground cloves
- 1 teaspoon ground cinnamon
- ½ teaspoon ground nutmeg
- ½ teaspoon salt
- ½ teaspoon baking soda
- 1 cup chopped nuts
- 1 cup confectioners' sugar
- 2 ½ tablespoons lemon juice

**Directions**

**Step 1**

Preheat oven to 350 degrees F (175 degrees C). Grease and flour a bundt pan or loaf pans.

**Step 2**

In a large bowl, mix together vegetable oil, white sugar, eggs, plum baby food, and food coloring. In a separate bowl, mix together flour, cloves, cinnamon, nutmeg, salt, baking soda, and nuts.

**Step 3**

Mix wet and dry ingredients together. Transfer batter to prepared pan(s).

**Step 4**

Bake in the preheated oven for 50-60 minutes or until a tester comes out clean. (Smaller loaf pans will take less time.)

**Step 5**

Remove from oven to cool 10 minutes in pan. Remove and place on cooling rack.

**Step 6**

While the cake is cooling, combine confectioners' sugar and lemon juice. Brush over top while cake is still hot.

**Nutrition Facts**

**Per Serving:**

384.5 calories; protein 4.3g 9% DV; carbohydrates 49.6g 16% DV; fat 19.9g 31% DV; cholesterol 34.9mg 12% DV; sodium 127.7mg 5% DV.

# Popcorn Cake

**Servings:** 16 **Yield:** 1 bundt cake

## Ingredients

- 4 quarts popped popcorn
- 1 pound candy-coated chocolate pieces
- 1 cup peanuts
- ⅓ cup vegetable oil
- ½ cup butter
- 1 pound marshmallows

## Directions

### Step 1

Mix popcorn, M&Ms, and peanuts in large bowl.

### Step 2

Heat oil, butter, and marshmallows in pan until melted. Pour over popcorn and blend together with heavy spoon or hands.

### Step 3

Spray Bundt cake pan with vegetable spray. Press mixture lightly into pan and refrigerate until cool.

### Step 4

To remove cake from pan, put pan in warm water, then turn upside down until cake comes out.

## Nutrition Facts

### Per Serving:

438.3 calories; protein 4.8g 10% DV; carbohydrates 50.2g 16% DV; fat 25.7g 40% DV; cholesterol 19.2mg 6% DV; sodium 197.1mg 8% DV.

# Gingerbread Cupcakes

**Prep:** 15 mins **Cook:** 15 mins **Total:** 30 mins **Servings:** 24 **Yield:** 24 cupcakes

## Ingredients

- 1 (18.25 ounce) box vanilla cake mix
- ½ cup buttermilk
- ½ cup molasses
- ⅓ cup vegetable oil
- 4 large eggs large eggs
- 1 ½ teaspoons ground ginger
- ½ teaspoon ground cinnamon
- ¼ teaspoon ground nutmeg

## Directions

### Step 1

Preheat oven to 350 degrees F (175 degrees C). Line 24 muffin cups with paper muffin liners.

### Step 2

Mix the cake mix, buttermilk, molasses, vegetable oil, eggs, ginger, cinnamon, and nutmeg together in large bowl until just combined. Spoon the batter into a large resealable plastic bag, press out excess air, and seal the top of the bag. Snip a corner of the bag about 1/4-inch from the bottom. Pipe the batter into the prepared muffin cups, filling them about 2/3 full.

### Step 3

Bake in the preheated oven until a toothpick inserted into the center comes out clean, 15 to 20 minutes. Cool in the pans for 10 minutes before removing to cool completely on a wire rack.

### Nutrition Facts

### Per Serving:

154.5 calories; protein 2.2g 4% DV; carbohydrates 22.4g 7% DV; fat 6.5g 10% DV; cholesterol 31.6mg 11% DV; sodium 161.1mg 6% DV.

# Easy Red Velvet Cake

**Prep:** 15 mins **Cook:** 25 mins **Total:** 40 mins **Servings:** 15 **Yield:** 1 9x13 inch cake

### Ingredients

- 1 (18.25 ounce) package white cake mix
- 1 (3.5 ounce) package non-instant chocolate pudding mix
- red food coloring, as desired
- ½ cup buttermilk

### Directions

### Step 1

Preheat oven to 350 degrees F (175 degrees C).

### Step 2

Prepare cake according to package directions, substituting half of the water called for with buttermilk (approximately 1/2 cup). Stir in pudding mix and food coloring.

### Step 3

Pour into cake pan(s) and bake according to package directions.

**Nutrition Facts**

**Per Serving:**

155.1 calories; protein 2g 4% DV; carbohydrates 28.2g 9% DV; fat 3.9g 6% DV; cholesterol 0.8mg; sodium 242.4mg 10% DV.

# Plum Pudding

**Prep:** 20 mins **Cook:** 2 hrs **Total:** 2 hrs 20 mins **Servings:** 6 **Yield:** 6 servings

## Ingredients

- ¼ cup butter
- ⅓ cup brown sugar
- 1 cup milk
- 12 dates dates, pitted and chopped
- ½ cup raisins
- ¼ cup dried currants

- ¼ cup candied mixed fruit peel, chopped
- 1 orange, zested
- 1 teaspoon baking soda
- 1 cup self-rising flour
- 2 teaspoons ground cinnamon
- 1 pinch salt

## Directions

### Step 1

Well grease a pudding mold.

### Step 2

In a large saucepan combine butter, sugar, milk, dates, raisins, currants, mixed fruit peel and zest of the orange; bring to a boil. Remove from heat and stir in baking soda. Sift in the flour, cinnamon and salt; mix gently until blended. Pour into prepared pudding mold.

### Step 3

Cover with a double layer of greased wax paper and steam for 2 hours.

**Nutrition Facts**

**Per Serving:**

307.6 calories; protein 4.2g 9% DV; carbohydrates 55.4g 18% DV; fat 8.8g 14% DV; cholesterol 23.6mg 8% DV; sodium 549.4mg 22% DV.

# Walnut-Cream Roll

**Prep:** 30 mins **Cook:** 15 mins **Additional:** 55 mins **Total:** 1 hr 40 mins **Servings:** 10 **Yield:** 1 roll

## Ingredients

- 4 large egg whites egg whites
- 1 teaspoon vanilla extract
- ½ teaspoon salt
- ½ cup white sugar
- 4 large egg yolks egg yolks
- ¼ cup sifted enriched flour

- ½ cup chopped walnuts
- 1 tablespoon sifted confectioners' sugar, or as needed
- 1 cup cold heavy cream
- 1 tablespoon white sugar, or to taste
- 1 tablespoon walnut halves, or as needed

## Directions

### Step 1

Preheat the oven to 375 degrees F (190 degrees C). Line the bottom and sides of a 15 1/2x10 1/2x1-inch jelly roll pan with waxed paper.

### Step 2

Beat egg whites, vanilla extract, and salt using an electric mixer in a mixing bowl until soft peaks form. Beat in 1/2 cup white sugar gradually until combined.

### Step 3

Beat egg yolks in a separate bowl using an electric mixer until thick and lemon-colored. Fold into egg white mixture. Fold in flour and chopped walnuts carefully until combined. Spread batter into the prepared jelly roll pan.

### Step 4

Bake in the preheated oven until cake springs back when lightly touched and a toothpick inserted into the center comes out clean, about 12 minutes.

### Step 5

Remove from the oven and let cool for 5 minutes. Loosen sides of cake; turn out onto a towel sprinkled with sifted confectioners' sugar. Peel off wax paper and let cool to lukewarm, 5 to 10 minutes.

### Step 6

Roll cake and towel together starting at the narrow end. Let cool completely on a wire rack, 15 to 20 minutes.

### Step 7

While cake cools, beat cold heavy cream and 1 tablespoon white sugar together in a mixing bowl using an electric mixer just until stiff peaks form.

**Step 8**

Unroll cake and spread with whipped cream, reserving some for topping. Re-roll cake and let chill in the refrigerator for at least 30 minutes. Top with dollops of whipped cream and walnut halves. Slice and serve.

**Nutrition Facts**

**Per Serving:**

212.7 calories; protein 4.3g 9% DV; carbohydrates 16.3g 5% DV; fat 15g 23% DV; cholesterol 114.5mg 38% DV; sodium 150.9mg 6% DV.

# Best Pumpkin Cheesecake

**Prep:** 20 mins **Cook:** 45 mins **Total:** 1 hr 5 mins **Servings:** 16 **Yield:** 2 - 9 inch pies

### Ingredients

- 3 (8 ounce) packages cream cheese
- 1 cup white sugar
- 1 cup sour cream
- 1 teaspoon vanilla extract

- 1 tablespoon pumpkin pie spice
- 6 large eggs eggs
- 1 cup pumpkin puree
- 2 (9 inch) prepared graham cracker crusts

### Directions

**Step 1**

Preheat oven to 375 degrees F (190 degrees C.)

**Step 2**

In a large bowl, beat cream cheese and sugar until smooth. Blend in sour cream, vanilla and spice. Beat in eggs, one at a time. Blend in pumpkin puree until no streaks remain. Pour filling into 2 crusts.

**Step 3**

Bake in the preheated oven for 45 minutes, or until filling is set. Allow to cool, then refrigerate at least 4 hours before serving.

**Nutrition Facts**

**Per Serving:**

407.3 calories; protein 7.4g 15% DV; carbohydrates 35.4g 11% DV; fat 27g 42% DV; cholesterol 122.3mg 41% DV; sodium 365.9mg 15% DV.

# Lemon Sunshine Cake

**Prep:** 15 mins **Cook:** 50 mins **Additional:** 1 hr **Total:** 2 hrs 5 mins **Servings:** 12 **Yield:** 1 10-inch fluted tube cake

## Ingredients

- 1 (18.25 ounce) package lemon cake mix
- 1 (3 ounce) package instant lemon pudding mix
- ½ cup white sugar
- 4 large eggs eggs
- 1 cup peach nectar
- ½ cup vegetable oil
- 2 cups sifted confectioners' sugar
- ¼ cup peach nectar
- 1 tablespoon lemon juice
- 1 teaspoon grated lemon peel

## Directions

### Step 1

Preheat oven to 350 degrees F (175 degrees C).

### Step 2

Grease and flour a 10-inch fluted tube pan (such as a Bundt).

### Step 3

Beat lemon cake mix, lemon pudding mix, white sugar, eggs, 1 cup peach nectar, and vegetable oil in a bowl with electric mixer on medium speed for 2 minutes.

### Step 4

Pour batter into prepared cake pan.

### Step 5

Bake in preheated oven until top of cake springs back when lightly pressed and a toothpick inserted into the middle of the cake comes out clean, about 50 minutes.

### Step 6

Cool cake in the pan for 15 minutes before removing cake to finish cooling on rack.

### Step 7

Mix confectioners' sugar, 1/4 cup peach nectar, lemon juice, and lemon peel in a bowl to make a smooth frosting.

### Step 8

Place cake on a serving platter; poke holes in top of the cake with a fork. Pour frosting slowly over the cake, allowing frosting to soak into the holes and drizzle down the sides of the cake.

### Nutrition Facts

### Per Serving:

445.1 calories; protein 4.7g 10% DV; carbohydrates 72.3g 23% DV; fat 16g 25% DV; cholesterol 73.1mg 24% DV; sodium 442.5mg 18% DV.

# Grandma's Suet Pudding

**Prep:** 10 mins **Cook:** 2 hrs **Total:** 2 hrs 10 mins **Servings:** 15 **Yield:** 15 servings

### Ingredients

- 1 cup milk
- 1 teaspoon lemon juice
- 1 cup chopped suet
- 1 cup molasses
- 1 teaspoon baking soda

- 2 cups all-purpose flour
- 1 cup raisins
- 1 egg white, beaten
- 9 tablespoons confectioners' sugar
- vanilla extract to taste

### Directions

### Step 1

Sour the milk by adding the lemon juice.

### Step 2

In a large bowl combine suet, molasses, soured milk, baking soda, flour and raisins. Place batter in a pudding mold or large double boiler and steam, uncovered, for 2 hours.

### Step 3

To make the sauce combine, in a small saucepan, the egg white, confectioner's sugar and vanilla. Heat over medium until thickened. Serve over warm pudding.

### Nutrition Facts

### Per Serving:

288.6 calories; protein 2.9g 6% DV; carbohydrates 40.6g 13% DV; fat 13.1g 20% DV; cholesterol 10.4mg 4% DV; sodium 104.6mg 4% DV.

# Grandma's Fruit Cake

**Prep:** 30 mins **Cook:** 1 hr 40 mins **Total:** 2 hrs 10 mins **Servings:** 20 **Yield:** 20 servings

## Ingredients

- 3 cups water
- 1 ½ cups raisins
- 3 cups all-purpose flour
- 2 tablespoons ground cinnamon
- 1 ½ tablespoons baking powder
- 1 tablespoon baking soda
- ½ teaspoon salt
- 1 pound pecan halves
- 2 tablespoons all-purpose flour
- 2 cups white sugar
- 1 ½ cups canola oil
- 4 large eggs eggs, beaten
- 3 cups candied fruit

## Directions

### Step 1

Preheat oven to 350 degrees F (175 degrees C). Grease two 8x8-inch baking pans.

### Step 2

Bring water and raisins to a boil in a saucepan; cook until raisins are plump, about 2 minutes. Drain and cool raisins; reserve raisin water.

### Step 3

Mix 3 cups flour, cinnamon, baking powder, baking soda, and salt together in a bowl. Place pecans and 2 tablespoons flour in a resealable plastic bag; close and shake bag until pecans are coated. Pour pecans into a colander and shake off excess flour.

### Step 4

Whisk sugar, oil, eggs, and cooled raisin water together in a bowl; fold in candied fruit. Stir flour mixture, 1/2 cup at a time, into sugar mixture until fully incorporated; fold in raisins and pecans. Fill the prepared pans a little over half full.

### Step 5

Bake in the preheated oven for 40 minutes. Lower temperature to 325 degrees F (165 degrees C); bake until a knife inserted in the center of the cake comes out clean, about 1 more hour.

## Nutrition Facts

620.5 calories; protein 5.8g 12% DV; carbohydrates 77.7g 25% DV; fat 34.5g 53% DV; cholesterol 37.2mg 12% DV; sodium 465.4mg 19% DV.

# Dundee Cake

**Servings: 12 Yield:** 1 cake

## Ingredients

- 1 cup raisins
- 1 cup dried currants
- ⅓ cup diced candies mixed fruit peel
- ⅓ cup candied cherries, quartered
- 2 tablespoons grated orange zest
- ⅓ cup all-purpose flour
- 1 cup butter, softened

- 1 cup white sugar
- 4 large eggs eggs
- 1 ⅔ cups all-purpose flour
- 1 teaspoon baking powder
- 1 ounce ground almonds
- ½ cup whole almonds
- 1 tablespoon corn syrup

## Directions

### Step 1

Combine raisins, currants, mixed peel, cherries, and orange rind. Dredge with 1/3 cup flour.

### Step 2

Cream butter or margarine and sugar until fluffy. Beat in eggs 1 at a time until light. Combine 1 2/3 cups flour, baking powder, and ground almonds; fold into batter mixture. Mix in fruit. Spread in foil lined 8 x 3 inch round pan. If using a different size pan fill 3/4 full.

### Step 3

Bake at 325 degrees F (165 degrees C) for about 1 1/2 hours, until an inserted wooden pick comes out clean. Remove cake from pan.

### Step 4

Toast almonds in 350 degrees F (175 degrees C) oven until lightly browned, about 5 minutes. Heat corn syrup, and brush over top surface of hot cake. Place almonds in whatever design you like. After cooling, cake will not be sticky.

## Nutrition Facts

## Per Serving:

456.1 calories; protein 7.1g 14% DV; carbohydrates 62.6g 20% DV; fat 21.5g 33% DV; cholesterol 102.7mg 34% DV; sodium 178.7mg 7% DV.

# Best Ever New Zealand Pavlova

**Prep:** 10 mins **Cook:** 45 mins **Total:** 55 mins **Servings:** 12 **Yield:** 1 - 9 inch meringue

## Ingredients

- 3 large egg whites egg whites
- 1 ¼ cups white sugar
- 2 tablespoons water
- 3 teaspoons cornstarch

- ½ teaspoon vanilla extract
- 1 teaspoon distilled white vinegar
- ⅛ teaspoon salt

## Directions

### Step 1

Preheat oven to 275 degrees F (135 degrees C). Grease a cookie sheet, line it with parchment paper and sprinkle a little water over paper.

### Step 2

In a large glass or metal mixing bowl, beat egg whites until foamy. Gradually add sugar, continuing to beat until stiff peaks form. Beat in water, then mix in cornstarch, vanilla, vinegar and salt.

### Step 3

Pour entire meringue mixture onto the center of the pan. Pavlova will spread as it bakes.

### Step 4

Bake in the preheated oven for 45 minutes. Turn oven off and leave Pavlova in the oven until cold. Turn upside-down onto plate and top with fresh fruit and whipped cream.

## Nutrition Facts

## Per Serving:

87.7 calories; protein 0.9g 2% DV; carbohydrates 21.5g 7% DV; fatg; cholesterolmg; sodium 38.2mg 2% DV.

# Streusel Coffee Cake

**Servings:** 12 **Yield:** 1 - 10 inch Bundt cake

## Ingredients

- 1 cup butter
- 2 cups white sugar
- 4 large eggs eggs
- 2 cups sour cream
- 2 teaspoons vanilla extract
- 4 cups all-purpose flour

- 2 teaspoons baking powder
- 2 teaspoons baking soda
- ½ cup white sugar
- 2 teaspoons ground cinnamon
- 1 cup chopped walnuts

## Directions

### Step 1

Preheat oven to 350 degrees F (175 degrees C). Grease and flour a 10 inch Bundt pan. In a medium bowl, mix the flour, baking powder and baking soda together and set aside. In a separate small bowl, combine 1/2 cup sugar, cinnamon, and nuts. Set aside.

### Step 2

In a large bowl, cream butter and 2 cups white sugar until light and fluffy. Add eggs, sour cream, and vanilla extract. Add flour mixture and beat until well combined.

### Step 3

Pour half of batter into Bundt pan. Sprinkle half of the nut mixture on top of batter in pan. Add remaining batter, and sprinkle with the last of the nut mixture.

### Step 4

Bake at 350 degrees F (175 degrees C) for 45 to 60 minutes, or until a toothpick inserted into cake comes out clean.

## Nutrition Facts

### Per Serving:

621.6 calories; protein 9.3g 19% DV; carbohydrates 77.2g 25% DV; fat 31.8g 49% DV; cholesterol 119.5mg 40% DV; sodium 444.8mg 18% DV.

# Holiday Bourbon Fruitcake

**Prep:** 35 mins **Cook:** 3 hrs 30 mins **Additional:** 2 days **Total:** 2 days **Servings:** 30 **Yield:** 2 - 9x5 inch loaves

## Ingredients

- 1 cup chopped candied orange peel
- 1 cup chopped candied citron
- 1 cup chopped candied pineapple
- 1 cup halved red candied cherries
- 1 cup halved green candied cherries
- 1 cup dried currants
- 1 cup raisins
- 1 cup chopped pitted dates
- 1 cup chopped walnuts
- ¾ cup chopped almonds
- ½ cup orange juice
- ⅔ cup bourbon whiskey
- 4 cups all-purpose flour
- 2 teaspoons ground cinnamon
- 2 teaspoons ground nutmeg

- 1 teaspoon ground cloves
- 1 teaspoon ground allspice
- 1 teaspoon ground ginger
- 2 teaspoons unsweetened cocoa powder
- 1 teaspoon baking powder
- ½ teaspoon salt
- 1 ½ cups butter, room temperature
- 1 cup packed brown sugar
- ½ cup white sugar
- 6 large egg yolks egg yolks
- ¾ cup applesauce
- ½ cup bourbon whiskey
- 1 teaspoon vanilla extract
- ½ cup molasses
- 6 large egg whites egg whites

## Directions

### Step 1

On the first day, combine the candied orange peel, candied citron, candied pineapple, red and green candied cherries, currants, raisins, walnuts, and almonds. Combine the orange juice and the 2/3 cup bourbon; pour over the fruit and nuts. Stir and then cover tightly. Let the fruit marinate in a cool place for 1 full day, or at least 20 hours.

### Step 2

On the second day, line two 9x5 inch loaf pans with parchment paper or aluminum foil and grease the inside with cooking spray. Combine the flour, cinnamon, nutmeg, cloves, allspice, ginger, cocoa, baking powder, and salt in a large bowl and stir with a whisk to blend.

### Step 3

In a separate large bowl, beat the butter, brown sugar, and white sugar until light and fluffy using an electric mixer. Stir in the egg yolks until blended and then mix in the applesauce, the 1/2 cup bourbon, and vanilla until fluffy. Continue stirring, and add the the flour mixture gradually until well combined.

Add the molasses and stir to combine. When the batter is thoroughly mixed, gently mix in the fruit and nut mixture with all of its juices.

**Step 4**

In a separate bowl, whip the egg whites with an electric mixer until they can hold a stiff peak. Fold egg whites into the batter. Divide evenly between the prepared pans. Cover loosely with a towel and let the batter stand overnight in a cool, dry place.

**Step 5**

On the third day, preheat the oven to 250 degrees F (120 degrees C). Place a large baking pan on the bottom shelf and pour boiling water into it until almost full. Place a baking sheet on the center shelf and place the fruit cakes on the baking sheet.

**Step 6**

Bake for 2 1/2 hours in the preheated oven. Check the water level and refill if needed. Cover the cakes with a sheet of parchment paper, taking care not to let it touch the shelf. Continue to bake until a knife or toothpick inserted into the center comes out clean, about 1 hour more. Cool fruitcakes in the pans, set over a wire rack. Once cool, remove the cakes from the pans, and leave the parchment paper on. Sprinkle with more bourbon if desired and wrap in aluminum foil. Place in a tin or other sealed container overnight before serving.

**Nutrition Facts**

**Per Serving:**

422.3 calories; protein 5.1g 10% DV; carbohydrates 64.9g 21% DV; fat 14.9g 23% DV; cholesterol 65.4mg 22% DV; sodium 172.1mg 7% DV.

# Upside Down Pear Gingerbread Cake

**Prep:** 20 mins **Cook:** 45 mins **Additional:** 1 hr **Total:** 2 hrs 5 mins **Servings:** 12 **Yield:** 1 10-inch cake

### Ingredients

- 2 ½ cups all-purpose flour
- 1 ½ teaspoons baking soda
- 2 teaspoons ground cinnamon
- 2 teaspoons ground ginger
- 1 teaspoon ground cloves
- ½ teaspoon salt
- ¼ cup butter

- ¼ cup brown sugar
- 1 (29 ounce) can pear halves, well drained
- ½ cup white sugar
- ½ cup butter, softened
- 1 egg
- 1 cup molasses
- 1 cup hot water

### Directions

**Step 1**

Preheat oven to 350 degrees F (175 degrees C). In a bowl, lightly mix the flour, baking soda, cinnamon, ginger, cloves, and salt until thoroughly combined.

**Step 2**

Place 1/4 cup of butter into a 10-inch springform pan, put it in the oven, and allow to melt for a minute or two. Sprinkle the melted butter evenly with brown sugar. Pat the pear halves dry with paper towels, and cut each half into 3 slices lengthwise. Arrange the pear slices in a spiral pattern on top of the brown sugar. Without disturbing the arranged slices, spray the inside walls of the pan with cooking spray.

**Step 3**

Beat the white sugar and 1/2 cup of butter in a mixing bowl with an electric mixer until creamy; beat in the egg, then mix in the molasses. Mix the flour mixture into the molasses mixture, then stir in the hot water. Pour the batter into the springform pan on top of the pear slices.

**Step 4**

Bake the cake in the preheated oven until a knife inserted into the cake comes out clean, 45 to 50 minutes.

**Step 5**

Allow to cool completely in the pan before inverting on a serving dish and removing pan.

**Nutrition Facts**

**Per Serving:**

368.3 calories; protein 3.6g 7% DV; carbohydrates 62.7g 20% DV; fat 12.3g 19% DV; cholesterol 46mg 15% DV; sodium 357.6mg 14% DV.

# Coconut Sour Cream Pound Cake

**Prep:** 15 mins **Cook:** 1 hr 20 mins **Total:** 1 hr 35 mins **Servings:** 15 **Yield:** 1 9-inch tube cake

**Ingredients**

- 1 cup vegetable shortening (such as Crisco)
- 3 cups white sugar
- 6 large eggs eggs
- 1 cup sour cream
- 3 cups sifted cake flour
- ¼ teaspoon baking soda
- 1 tablespoon coconut extract

**Directions**

**Step 1**

Preheat oven to 300 degrees F (150 degrees C). Grease and flour a 9-inch tube pan.

**Step 2**

Beat vegetable shortening and sugar together in a bowl using an electric mixer until mixture is creamy. Beat eggs into shortening mixture, one at a time, letting each egg blend in before adding the next. Beat in sour cream until smooth.

**Step 3**

Gradually stir cake flour and baking soda into the moist ingredients until batter is smooth; stir in coconut extract. Scoop batter into prepared tube pan.

**Step 4**

Bake in the preheated oven until a toothpick inserted into the middle of the cake comes out clean or with moist crumbs, 1 hour and 20 minutes.

**Nutrition Facts**

**Per Serving:**

442.7 calories; protein 5.3g 11% DV; carbohydrates 63.2g 20% DV; fat 19.1g 29% DV; cholesterol 81.1mg 27% DV; sodium 57.7mg 2% DV.

# Apple-Pecan Cheesecake

**Prep:** 30 mins **Cook:** 55 mins **Additional:** 4 hrs 30 mins **Total:** 5 hrs 55 mins **Servings:** 16 **Yield:** 16 servings

**Ingredients**

**Crust**

- 1 ½ cups graham cracker crumbs
- ¼ cup melted butter
- 2 tablespoons packed brown sugar

**Filling**

- 4 (8 ounce) packages cream cheese, softened
- 1 cup packed brown sugar
- 1 teaspoon vanilla extract

- 1 cup sour cream
- 4 large eggs eggs

**Topping**

- 4 cups apples (about 3) - peeled, cored, and chopped
- ½ cup packed brown sugar
- ¾ cup chopped pecans
- 1 teaspoon ground cinnamon

**Directions**

### Step 1

Preheat oven to 325 degrees F (165 degrees C). Line a 9x13 inch baking dish with aluminum foil, extending the foil sheets over the side of the dish.

### Step 2

To make the crust, mix the graham cracker crumbs, butter, and 2 tablespoons brown sugar together in a bowl until evenly blended. Press evenly over the bottom of the prepared baking dish.

### Step 3

To make the filling, beat the cream cheese, 1 cup brown sugar, and vanilla together in a mixing bowl until evenly blended. Beat in the sour cream. On low speed, add the eggs, one at a time, just until blended. Pour the mixture over the crust.

### Step 4

To make the topping, place the apples in a bowl, and toss with 1/2 cup brown sugar, pecans, and cinnamon until evenly blended.

### Step 5

Bake in preheated oven until center is almost set, about 55 minutes. Cool, and refrigerate 4 hours, or overnight.

### Step 6

Before cutting, allow the cheesecake to sit 30 minutes at room temperature, then lift from the baking dish using the extended aluminum foil sheets, and place on a cutting board or serving plate. Remove the aluminum foil, and cut into 16 squares.

**Nutrition Facts**

**Per Serving:**

456.2 calories; protein 7.7g 15% DV; carbohydrates 37.1g 12% DV; fat 32.1g 49% DV; cholesterol 122.1mg 41% DV; sodium 263.2mg 11% DV.

# Christmas Plum Pudding

**Prep:** 30 mins **Cook:** 5 hrs **Total:** 5 hrs 30 mins **Servings:** 20 **Yield:** 20 servings

## Ingredients

- 1 cup whole wheat flour
- 2 ½ cups fresh bread crumbs
- 4 ounces shredded suet
- 3 large eggs eggs, beaten
- 1 small carrot, grated
- 1 apple - peeled, cored and shredded
- ½ cup dark brown sugar
- ½ cup chopped blanched almonds
- 2 ounces preserved stem ginger in syrup, chopped
- ⅛ cup ground almonds
- ½ cup chopped walnuts
- ⅜ cup halved candied cherries
- ⅓ cup raisins
- ⅜ cup dried currants
- ⅜ cup golden raisins
- 4 ounces candied mixed fruit peel, chopped
- 4 fruit (2-1/8" dia)s plums, pitted and chopped
- 1 lemon, juiced and zested
- 1 ½ teaspoons mixed spice
- ¾ teaspoon baking powder
- ½ cup ale

## Directions

### Step 1

In a large bowl, combine flour, bread crumbs, suet, eggs, carrot, apple, brown sugar, chopped blanched almonds, stem ginger, ground almonds, cherries, raisins, currants, golden raisins, mixed peel, plums, lemon juice and zest, mixed spice, baking powder and ale. Let each family member take a turn stirring and make a wish. If you have used more dry fruit than fresh, add a little extra ale to make the mixture less stiff.

### Step 2

Grease 2 large or 4 small pudding basins. Fill with pudding mixture about 7/8 full. Cover tightly with greased waxed paper, then foil; secure with string. Stand pudding on a trivet in a large pot of boiling water that reaches halfway up the sides of the pudding basin. Steam puddings over medium-low heat in boiling water 10 hours for large puddings, 5 hours for small puddings, topping off water regularly until quite firm and set.

### Step 3

If not serving immediately, let cool completely, then replace covers with fresh waxed paper and foil and store in a cool, dry place, basting from time to time with rum or brandy, for up to 3 months. To serve, reheat by steaming 2 to 3 hours.

**Nutrition Facts**

Per Serving:

228.4 calories; protein 4.1g 8% DV; carbohydrates 32g 10% DV; fat 10.4g 16% DV; cholesterol 31.8mg 11% DV; sodium 69.4mg 3% DV.

# Cranberry Sour Cream Kuchen

**Prep:** 20 mins **Cook:** 50 mins **Total:** 1 hr 10 mins **Servings:** 12 **Yield:** 1 10-inch cake

## Ingredients

- ½ cup butter
- 1 cup white sugar
- 1 teaspoon vanilla extract
- 3 large eggs eggs
- 2 cups all-purpose flour
- 2 teaspoons baking powder
- ½ teaspoon baking soda
- ½ teaspoon salt

- 1 ¼ cups sour cream
- 2 cups chopped fresh cranberries
- ¼ cup white sugar
- ¼ cup brown sugar
- 2 tablespoons all-purpose flour
- 2 tablespoons chopped almonds
- 1 tablespoon butter
- ½ teaspoon ground cinnamon

## Directions

### Step 1

Preheat oven to 350 degrees F (175 degrees C). Grease a 10-inch springform pan.

### Step 2

Beat 1/2 cup butter, 1 cup white sugar, and vanilla extract in a large bowl using an electric mixer until creamy and smooth. Add eggs, 1 at a time, beating in the first egg thoroughly before adding the second. Whisk 2 cups flour, baking powder, baking soda, and salt together in a separate bowl; beat flour mixture into creamed butter mixture in several increments, alternating with sour cream, to make a batter.

### Step 3

Spread half the batter in the prepared pan. Combine cranberries with 1/4 cup white sugar in a bowl and spread the cranberries over batter; top with remaining batter. Stir brown sugar, 2 tablespoons flour, almonds, 1 tablespoon butter, and cinnamon together in a bowl until the topping looks like crumbs. Sprinkle topping evenly over cake.

### Step 4

Bake in the preheated oven until the cake is lightly browned and a toothpick inserted into the center comes out clean or with moist crumbs, 50 to 55 minutes.

## Nutrition Facts

**Per Serving:**

339.9 calories; protein 5g 10% DV; carbohydrates 46.1g 15% DV; fat 15.6g 24% DV; cholesterol 79.9mg 27% DV; sodium 324.2mg 13% DV.

# Almond Pound Cake

**Prep:** 1 hr **Cook:** 1 hr **Total:** 2 hrs **Servings:** 12 **Yield:** 1 - 10 inch Bundt cake

### Ingredients

- 1 cup butter, softened
- 2 cups white sugar
- 6 large eggs eggs, room temperature
- 1 ¾ cups all-purpose flour
- ½ teaspoon salt
- 2 teaspoons almond extract

- 8 ounces almond paste
- 1 cup confectioners' sugar
- 4 tablespoons milk
- ½ cup blanched almonds
- 4 drops red food coloring
- 4 drops green food coloring

### Directions

### Step 1

Preheat oven to 325 degrees F (165 degrees C). Grease and flour a 10 inch Bundt pan.

### Step 2

In a large bowl, cream butter and sugar together until well mixed with an electric mixer. Add eggs, one at a time, and beat until mixture is light and fluffy. Blend in flour and salt. Mix in almond extract. Turn batter into prepared pan.

### Step 3

Bake for 60 minutes, or until a toothpick when inserted in the center of the cake comes out clean. Cool in pan for 10 minutes. Remove from pan, and transfer to a wire rack to continue cooling.

### Step 4

Break off tablespoon-sized pieces of the almond paste, and shape into holly leaves. Using the tip of a knife, score the shaped holly leaf to resemble veins in the leaves. Mix green food coloring with a small amount of water and brush the holly leaves, repeating until desired color is reached. Set aside on waxed paper. Break off 2 tablespoons of almond paste, and knead in several drops of red food coloring. When color of almond paste is a bright red, break off smaller pieces. Roll into balls to resemble holly berries. Place on waxed paper.

### Step 5

In a small bowl, combine 1 cup confectioners' sugar and milk. Mix until smooth. When the cake has cooled, drizzle with the confectioners' sugar glaze. Top with blanched almonds, and garnish with the marzipan holly leaves and berries.

**Nutrition Facts**

**Per Serving:**

531 calories; protein 8.3g 17% DV; carbohydrates 67.8g 22% DV; fat 26.4g 41% DV; cholesterol 134.1mg 45% DV; sodium 245.2mg 10% DV.

# Beer Spice Cake

**Prep:** 15 mins **Cook:** 50 mins **Total:** 1 hr 5 mins **Servings:** 12 **Yield:** 1 - 9x5 inch loaf pan

## Ingredients

- 1 ½ cups all-purpose flour
- 1 teaspoon baking powder
- 1 teaspoon ground cloves
- 1 teaspoon ground cinnamon
- 1 teaspoon ground allspice
- ½ teaspoon baking soda
- ¼ teaspoon salt
- ½ cup butter or margarine, softened
- 1 cup brown sugar
- 1 egg, beaten
- 1 cup beer
- 1 cup chopped walnuts

## Directions

### Step 1

Preheat oven to 375 degrees F (190 degrees C). Grease and flour a 9x5 inch loaf pan.

### Step 2

Sift together flour, baking powder, cloves, cinnamon, allspice, baking soda, and salt in a bowl. Set aside.

### Step 3

In a large bowl, cream the butter and brown sugar until light and fluffy. Add egg and beat well. Add flour mixture alternately with beer and mix well to combine. Fold in the chopped walnuts.

### Step 4

Pour into a 9x5 inch loaf pan. Bake 40 to 50 minutes in the preheated oven, or until a toothpick inserted into the cake comes out clean.

**Nutrition Facts**

**Per Serving:**

276.4 calories; protein 3.9g 8% DV; carbohydrates 32.5g 11% DV; fat 14.8g 23% DV; cholesterol 35.8mg 12% DV; sodium 198.5mg 8% DV.

# Icelandic Christmas Cake

**Servings: 15 Yield:** 1 -11 inch loaf pan

## Ingredients

- 1 cup white sugar
- ¾ cup butter
- 2 large eggs eggs
- 2 ½ cups all-purpose flour
- 2 teaspoons baking powder
- ¾ cup milk
- ½ cup raisins
- ½ teaspoon lemon extract
- ½ teaspoon cardamom flavored extract

## Directions

### Step 1

Preheat oven to 350 degrees F (175 degrees C). Grease one 11 inch loaf pan.

### Step 2

Cream the butter or margarine and the sugar until light and fluffy. Add the eggs one at time beating well after each one. Stir in the milk, lemon and cardamom flavorings. Stir in the flour and the baking powder.

### Step 3

Sift a little flour over the raisins then stir them into the batter. Pour the batter into the prepared pan.

### Step 4

Bake at 350 degrees F (175 degrees C) for 55 to 60 minutes.

## Nutrition Facts

### Per Serving:

240.4 calories; protein 3.6g 7% DV; carbohydrates 33.9g 11% DV; fat 10.3g 16% DV; cholesterol 50.2mg 17% DV; sodium 145.7mg 6% DV.

# Chocolate Plum Pudding Cake

**Prep:** 25 mins **Cook:** 1 hr 20 mins **Total:** 1 hr 45 mins **Servings:** 12 **Yield:** 1 - 9 inch tube cake

## Ingredients

- ⅔ cup raisins
- ¾ cup all-purpose flour
- ¾ cup whole wheat flour
- ⅓ cup unsweetened cocoa powder
- 2 teaspoons baking soda
- ¼ teaspoon salt
- 1 tablespoon ground cinnamon
- ½ teaspoon ground nutmeg
- ¾ cup butter, softened
- 1 ½ cups white sugar
- 3 large eggs eggs
- 2 cups applesauce
- ½ cup coarsely chopped walnuts

## Directions

### Step 1

Preheat oven to 350 degrees F (175 degrees C). Place raisins in a small saucepan, and cover with boiling water. Soak for 5 minutes, then drain. Grease and flour a 9 inch tube pan.

### Step 2

Sift together the all-purpose flour, whole wheat flour, cocoa, baking soda, salt, cinnamon, and nutmeg. Set aside.

### Step 3

In a large bowl, cream butter and sugar until light and fluffy. Blend in the eggs, then the applesauce. Beat in the flour mixture. Stir in raisins and walnuts. Spread batter evenly into prepared tube pan.

### Step 4

Bake in preheated oven for 80 minutes, or until a toothpick inserted in the center of cake comes out clean. Let cool in pan for 10 minutes, then turn out onto a wire rack and cool completely; chill.

## Nutrition Facts

### Per Serving:

351.2 calories; protein 5.1g 10% DV; carbohydrates 50g 16% DV; fat 16.6g 26% DV; cholesterol 77mg 26% DV; sodium 360.3mg 14% DV.

# Deep Dark Chocolate Peppermint Cake

**Prep:** 30 mins **Cook:** 30 mins **Additional:** 1 hr 30 mins **Total:** 2 hrs 30 mins **Servings:** 12 **Yield:** 1 9-inch layer cake

## Ingredients

- 2 cups sifted cake flour
- ¾ teaspoon salt
- 4 (1 ounce) squares unsweetened chocolate
- ¼ cup butter
- 2 cups white sugar
- 2 large egg yolks egg yolks
- 1 ¾ cups milk, divided
- 1 teaspoon vanilla extract
- 1 teaspoon baking soda
- Seven-Minute Frosting
- ½ cup crushed peppermint hard candies
- 3 drops red food coloring

## Directions

### Step 1

Preheat oven to 350 degrees F (175 degrees C). Grease two 9-inch round pans and line the bottoms with parchment paper.

### Step 2

Sift together the cake flour and salt.

### Step 3

Melt chocolate and butter together in a double boiler. Turn into mixing bowl, and cool to room temperature; this mixture must be cool. Mix in the sugar. Blend in egg yolks and 1 cup milk.

### Step 4

Pour in the flour and salt, and mix just until incorporated. Beat batter with electric mixer for 1 minute, and then blend in vanilla and 1/2 cup milk. Dissolve baking soda in the remaining 1/4 cup milk; stir into the batter quickly and thoroughly. Pour batter into prepared pans.

### Step 5

Bake in the preheated oven until the surface of the cakes spring back lightly when pressed with a finger, about 30 minutes. Cool cakes on wire racks.

### Step 6

Prepare Seven Minute Frosting, omitting vanilla (see Footnote for link). Tint the frosting a delicate pink with a few drops of food coloring, and add 1/4 cup crushed candy. Frost and fill the cooled cake. Garnish with bits of crushed candy.

76

## Nutrition Facts

**Per Serving:**

362.9 calories; protein 4.8g 10% DV; carbohydrates 66.3g 21% DV; fat 10.4g 16% DV; cholesterol 47.2mg 16% DV; sodium 300.1mg 12% DV.

# Plum Pudding

**Prep:** 15 mins **Cook:** 55 mins **Total:** 1 hr 10 mins **Servings:** 8 **Yield:** 8 servings

## Ingredients

- ½ cup butter, room temperature
- 1 cup white sugar
- 6 large eggs eggs, room temperature
- ½ cup chopped candied citron
- 1 ½ cups pitted prunes, chopped
- ½ cup raisins
- 1 cup coarsely chopped pecans
- ½ cup all-purpose flour
- 1 ½ cups fine dry bread crumbs
- 1 teaspoon ground cinnamon
- 1 teaspoon ground nutmeg
- ½ teaspoon ground allspice

## Directions

### Step 1

Preheat oven to 350 degrees F (175 degrees C). Grease and flour a 2 quart souffle or casserole dish.

### Step 2

In a large bowl, cream together the butter and sugar until light and fluffy. Beat in the eggs one at a time.

### Step 3

In a separate bowl combine the citron, prunes, raisins and pecans. Stir in the flour and toss so that everything is coated with flour.

### Step 4

To the butter mixture add the fruit and nut mixture along with the bread crumbs, cinnamon, nutmeg and allspice. Mix well and transfer to prepared dish.

### Step 5

Bake in preheated oven for 50 to 55 minutes, or until well browned.

## Nutrition Facts

**Per Serving:**

566.9 calories; protein 10.2g 20% DV; carbohydrates 76.7g 25% DV; fat 26.5g 41% DV; cholesterol 170mg 57% DV; sodium 327.8mg 13% DV.

# Cranberry Pudding

**Prep:** 25 mins **Cook:** 1 hr **Additional:** 20 mins **Total:** 1 hr 45 mins **Servings:** 10 **Yield:** 10 to 12 servings

## Ingredients

- 2 cups cranberries
- 1 ½ cups all-purpose flour
- ½ teaspoon salt
- ½ teaspoon baking soda
- ⅓ cup boiling water
- ½ cup molasses
- 1 cup white sugar
- ½ cup butter, softened
- ½ cup heavy whipping cream
- 1 teaspoon vanilla extract

## Directions

### Step 1

Lightly grease a 2-quart metal pudding mold or a clean 1-pound coffee can. Pick over whole cranberries; wash and drain.

### Step 2

Sift together the flour and salt; dredge cranberries in flour mixture.

### Step 3

Dissolve soda into boiling water and add molasses. Stir and allow to foam up.

### Step 4

Add to the flour and cranberry mixture. Mix together until well blended. Spoon into prepared mold or pan; cover with a double layer of aluminum foil and fasten with heavy elastic band or string.

### Step 5

Place into a deep saucepan and fill with water up to about the halfway mark on the pudding can. Cover saucepan and place over high heat. Bring water to boil, reduce heat, and simmer for 1 hour. Remove from water and allow to cool.

### Step 6

Prepare the sauce by mixing together the sugar, butter and cream. Cook over medium heat until thick, stirring constantly. Remove from heat and add vanilla.

**Step 7**

When ready to serve the pudding, invert pan or open bottom of can and push through. Slice in 1/2-inch pieces. Pour sauce over individual slices of pudding.

**Nutrition Facts**

**Per Serving:**

327 calories; protein 2.4g 5% DV; carbohydrates 49.6g 16% DV; fat 13.8g 21% DV; cholesterol 40.7mg 14% DV; sodium 256.3mg 10% DV.

# Eggnog Cheesecake

**Prep:** 20 mins **Cook:** 3 hrs **Total:** 3 hrs 20 mins **Servings:** 12 **Yield:** 1 cheesecake

## Ingredients

- 1 cup graham cracker crumbs
- 3 tablespoons white sugar
- 3 tablespoons butter, melted
- 4 (8 ounce) packages cream cheese, softened
- 1 cup white sugar
- 3 tablespoons all-purpose flour
- 4 large eggs eggs
- 1 cup eggnog
- 1 teaspoon vanilla extract

## Directions

**Step 1**

Lightly grease a 9-inch springform pan. Combine the graham cracker crumbs, 3 tablespoons white sugar, and butter in a bowl and mix until evenly moistened; press into the bottom of the prepared pan.

**Step 2**

Cream together the cream cheese and 1 cup sugar using an electric mixer. Add the flour and beat until smooth. Mix in the eggs with the mixer switched to low. Pour in the eggnog and vanilla; continue beating until just blended. Stop the mixer and scrape the bottom of the bowl occasionally. Pour the mixture over the crust.

**Step 3**

Fill a shallow dish with some hot water and place on bottom rack of the oven. Put cheesecake on the middle rack of the oven. Turn oven heat to 200 degrees F (95 degrees C). Do not preheat oven.

**Step 4**

Bake the cheesecake until the center is set, about 3 hours 15 minutes. Turn oven off. Allow cheesecake to cool in the oven, about 3 hours. Chill in refrigerator overnight.

**Nutrition Facts**

**Per Serving:**

452.8 calories; protein 9.3g 19% DV; carbohydrates 31.7g 10% DV; fat 32.9g 51% DV; cholesterol 164.3mg 55% DV; sodium 318.6mg 13% DV.

# Chocolate Bar Torte

**Prep:** 30 mins **Cook:** 5 mins **Additional:** 2 hrs **Total:** 2 hrs 35 mins **Servings:** 16 **Yield:** 1 9x13-inch pan

## Ingredients

- 1 cup milk
- 2 tablespoons milk
- 48 regulars large marshmallows, chopped
- 8 (1.55 ounce) bars chocolate candy (such as Hershey's)
- 3 cups heavy whipping cream
- 30 large rectangular piece or 2 squares or 4 small rectangular pieces graham cracker squares, crushed
- ¼ cup white sugar
- 6 tablespoons butter, melted

## Directions

### Step 1

Pour both amounts of milk into a saucepan, place over medium heat, and bring milk almost to a simmer, stirring often. Add marshmallows and chocolate candy bars. Stir until marshmallows and chocolate melt and the mixture is smooth. Set aside to cool.

### Step 2

Whip cream in a large bowl until fluffy and cream holds stiff peaks when beaters are lifted straight up, about 5 minutes. Gently fold cooled marshmallow mixture into whipped cream.

### Step 3

Combine graham cracker crumbs, sugar, and butter until crust mixture is evenly moist. Press mixture into the bottom of a 9x13-inch dish. Spread marshmallow filling evenly over the crumb crust. Refrigerate until set, about 2 hours.

**Nutrition Facts**

**Per Serving:**

472.8 calories; protein 4.5g 9% DV; carbohydrates 52.4g 17% DV; fat 28.6g 44% DV; cholesterol 77.6mg 26% DV; sodium 239.9mg 10% DV.

# Excellent Apple Gingerbread

**Prep:** 50 mins **Cook:** 40 mins **Additional:** 2 hrs **Total:** 3 hrs 30 mins **Servings:** 8 **Yield:** 1 9-inch layer cake

## Ingredients

- ¼ cup butter
- 3 eaches Granny Smith apples - peeled, cored and chopped
- ¾ cup butter at room temperature
- 1 tablespoon honey
- ½ cup white sugar
- ½ cup packed brown sugar
- 2 large eggs eggs
- 2 cups all-purpose flour
- 2 teaspoons baking soda
- 2 teaspoons ground cinnamon
- 1 teaspoon pumpkin pie spice
- 1 teaspoon ground cloves
- ½ teaspoon ground ginger
- ¼ teaspoon salt
- ½ cup milk
- ½ cup chopped walnuts
- 1 egg white
- 1 teaspoon ground cinnamon
- ½ cup chopped walnuts
- 1 tablespoon brown sugar
- ½ cup butter, softened
- 1 cup confectioners' sugar
- 1 (8 ounce) package cream cheese, softened
- 1 teaspoon vanilla extract
- 1 (20 ounce) can apple pie filling

## Directions

### Step 1

Melt 1/4 cup of butter in a large skillet over medium heat. Add the apples; cook and stir until tender. Set aside and allow to cool.

### Step 2

Preheat the oven to 350 degrees F (175 degrees C). Grease and flour two 9 inch round cake pans.

### Step 3

In a large bowl, mix 3/4 cup of butter, honey, brown sugar and white sugar until light and fluffy using an electric mixer. Beat in the eggs one at a time, mixing each one until blended. Combine the flour, baking soda, cinnamon, pumpkin pie spice, cloves, ginger and salt; stir into the batter, alternating with the milk. Stir in the walnuts and cooked apples just until evenly distributed. Divide evenly between the prepared pans and spread evenly.

### Step 4

Bake the cake in the preheated oven until a toothpick inserted in the center comes out clean, about 30 minutes. Cool the cakes on a wire rack. Keep the oven on for the walnuts.

## Step 5

To make the candied walnuts for the top of the cake, whip the egg whites in a clean bowl until foamy. Stir in the brown sugar, cinnamon and walnuts. Spread the nuts out on a baking sheet.

## Step 6

Bake in the preheated oven until toasted and fragrant, about 10 minutes. Cool completely before using.

## Step 7

To make the frosting, mix together the butter, confectioners' sugar and cream cheese until smooth. Place one layer of cake on a serving plate and spread with a thin layer of the cream cheese icing. Top with most of the apple filling and spread evenly. Place the other layer of cake on top with the bottom facing up. Spread remaining cream cheese icing over the top and sides. Decorate the top with remaining apple filling and sprinkle with candied walnuts.

## Nutrition Facts

### Per Serving:

918.4 calories; protein 10.8g 22% DV; carbohydrates 99.1g 32% DV; fat 56.1g 86% DV; cholesterol 170mg 57% DV; sodium 784.2mg 31% DV.

# Fruit Cake

**Prep:** 20 mins **Cook:** 1 hr 15 mins **Additional:** 1 hr **Total:** 2 hrs 35 mins **Servings:** 12 **Yield:** 1 9-inch tube cake

## Ingredients

- 1 serving cooking spray with flour
- 1 (18.25 ounce) package lemon cake mix (such as Duncan Hines Lemon Supreme)
- 4 large eggs eggs
- ½ cup vegetable oil
- 1 (3 ounce) package instant lemon pudding mix

- 1 tablespoon lemon extract
- 1 tablespoon vanilla extract
- 8 ounces candied red cherries, halved
- 8 ounces candied pineapple slices, cut into thirds
- 1 ½ cups chopped pecans
- 1 cup sweetened dried cranberries

## Directions

## Step 1

Preheat oven to 325 degrees F (165 degrees C). Spray a 9-inch fluted tube pan, such as a Bundt, with cooking spray.

## Step 2

Mix the cake mix, eggs, vegetable oil, lemon pudding mix, lemon extract, and vanilla extract together in a large bowl until smooth, and stir in candied cherries, pineapple, pecans, and dried cranberries. Pour the batter into the prepared cake pan.

## Step 3

Bake in the preheated oven until a toothpick inserted into the center of the cake comes out clean, about 1 hour and 15 minutes. Allow to cool in the pan for 20 minutes before turning it out onto a cake plate to finish cooling. Store in a covered container to help retain moisture.

## Nutrition Facts

## Per Serving:

547.7 calories; protein 5.9g 12% DV; carbohydrates 75g 24% DV; fat 25.7g 40% DV; cholesterol 73.1mg 24% DV; sodium 465.1mg 19% DV.

# Fluffy Pumpkin Spiced Cupcakes

**Prep:** 15 mins **Cook:** 30 mins **Additional:** 1 hr **Total:** 1 hr 45 mins **Servings:** 24 **Yield:** 2 dozen

## Ingredients

- 1 (15 ounce) can pumpkin puree
- 1 ½ cups white sugar
- 1 cup packed brown sugar
- ½ cup butter-flavored shortening
- ½ cup butter, softened
- ¼ cup whole milk
- ¼ cup vegetable oil
- 4 large eggs eggs
- 2 cups cake flour
- ¼ cup dry buttermilk powder
- ¼ cup cornstarch
- 2 teaspoons pumpkin pie spice
- 2 teaspoons baking powder
- 1 teaspoon baking soda
- ¾ teaspoon salt

## Directions

## Step 1

Preheat oven to 350 degrees F (175 degrees C). Line 24 muffin cups with paper muffin liners.

## Step 2

Beat the pumpkin puree, white sugar, brown sugar, shortening, butter, milk, vegetable oil, and eggs together in a large bowl until smooth. Whisk the cake flour, dry buttermilk powder, cornstarch, pumpkin pie spice, baking powder, baking soda, and salt together in another bowl. Add the dry ingredients to the pumpkin mixture, stirring until mixed. Pour batter into the prepared muffin cups, filling each cup about 2/3 full.

**Step 3**

Bake in the preheated until the center of the cupcakes spring back when touched, about 30 minutes. Cool in the pans for 10 minutes before removing to cool completely on a wire rack.

**Nutrition Facts**

**Per Serving:**

249.9 calories; protein 2.8g 6% DV; carbohydrates 34.5g 11% DV; fat 11.7g 18% DV; cholesterol 42.3mg 14% DV; sodium 257.9mg 10% DV.

# Flourless Chocolate Espresso Cake

**Prep:** 30 mins **Additional:** 2 hrs 40 mins **Total:** 3 hrs 10 mins **Servings:** 16 **Yield:** 16 servings

**Ingredients**

**Cake:**

- 1 tablespoon instant espresso powder
- 1 tablespoon hot water
- ¾ cup LAND O LAKES Unsalted Butter
- 6 ounces high-quality bittersweet chocolate baking bar, broken into small pieces

- 1 cup sugar
- 3 eaches LAND O LAKES Eggs
- ½ cup unsweetened cocoa powder

**Espresso Whipped Cream:**

- 1 teaspoon instant espresso powder
- 1 teaspoon hot water
- 1 cup LAND O LAKES Heavy Whipping Cream, chilled

- ¼ cup sugar
- 2 tablespoons powdered sugar
- ⅛ teaspoon extra fine edible glitter

**Directions**

**Step 1**

Heat oven to 350 degrees F.

**Step 2**

Wrap outside of 9-inch springform pan with aluminum foil. Line bottom of pan with parchment paper. Butter parchment paper and sides of pan.

**Step 3**

Combine 1 tablespoon instant espresso powder and 1 tablespoon hot water in bowl; set aside.

**Step 4**

Place butter and chocolate in 2-quart nonstick saucepan. Cook over medium heat, stirring occasionally, until melted. Remove from heat; stir in espresso mixture. Add sugar; beat with whisk until combined. Add 1 egg at a time, whisking after each addition. Whisk in cocoa until well mixed.

**Step 5**

Pour cake into prepared pan. Place springform pan into center of large roasting pan. Place roasting pan in oven. Fill space around springform pan slowly with hot water, to about 1 inch up sides of pan. Bake 40-45 minutes or until center of cake is set.

**Step 6**

Remove springform pan from roasting pan. Place onto cooling rack; remove foil. Cool completely.

**Step 7**

Combine 1 teaspoon instant espresso powder and 1 teaspoon hot water in bowl; set aside.

**Step 8**

Beat chilled whipping cream and 1/4 cup sugar in chilled bowl at high speed, scraping bowl often, until stiff peaks form. Stir in espresso mixture.

**Step 9**

Combine powdered sugar and edible glitter in bowl.

**Step 10**

Remove sides from springform pan; place cake onto serving plate. Place snowflake stencil on top of cake (see Recipe Tips). Lightly dust top of cake with powdered sugar mixture. Carefully remove stencil.

**Step 11**

Serve with espresso whipped cream.

**Nutrition Facts**

**Per Serving:**

273.9 calories; protein 2.8g 6% DV; carbohydrates 24.6g 8% DV; fat 19.4g 30% DV; cholesterol 79.8mg 27% DV; sodium 21.6mg 1% DV.

# Hazelnut and Chipped Chocolate Cheesecake

**Prep:** 5 mins **Cook:** 10 mins **Total:** 15 mins **Servings:** 12 **Yield:** 1 - 9 inch cheesecake

## Ingredients

- 2 cups semisweet chocolate chips
- 1 ½ cups vanilla wafer crumbs
- ¾ cup toasted, ground hazelnuts
- 2 tablespoons white sugar
- 3 tablespoons butter, melted
- 3 (8 ounce) packages cream cheese, softened

- 1 cup white sugar
- 3 large eggs eggs, beaten
- 3 tablespoons hazelnut liqueur
- 13 nuts skinned, toasted hazelnuts
- 4 tablespoons sour cream
- 1 tablespoon hazelnut liqueur

## Directions

### Step 1

Using a blender or a food processor, finely chop 1/3 cup semisweet chocolate chips. Place in a small mixing bowl. Add vanilla wafer crumbs, ground hazelnuts, 2 tablespoons white sugar, and melted butter or margarine. Mix until well combined. Press onto the bottom and up the sides of a 9 inch springform pan. Bake in a preheated 300 degrees F (150 degrees C) oven for 15 minutes. Cool.

### Step 2

In a large bowl, beat the cream cheese until fluffy. Gradually add 1 cup white sugar; mix well. Add the eggs and 3 tablespoons liqueur. Mix until well blended. Coarsely chop 1 cup of the semisweet chocolate chips, and add to the cream cheese mixture. Stir. Pour batter into the cooled crust.

### Step 3

Bake in a preheated 350 degrees F (175 degrees C) oven for 1 hour. Let cake cool for 1 hour. Remove outer ring from pan. Then let cool completely.

### Step 4

Melt 2/3 cup semisweet chocolate chips over hot (not boiling) water. Stir until smooth. Dip 13 hazelnuts into the chocolate, covering one-half of each nut. Shake off the excess chocolate. Place on a waxed-paper lined plate. Chill until set.

### Step 5

To the remaining melted chocolate, add sour cream. Mix well. Stir in 1 tablespoon liqueur. Spread glaze on top of the cooled cheesecake. Garnish with chocolate dipped hazelnuts.

## Nutrition Facts

**Per Serving:**

706.6 calories; protein 10.6g 21% DV; carbohydrates 68g 22% DV; fat 43.7g 67% DV; cholesterol 117.8mg 39% DV; sodium 275.4mg 11% DV.

# Extra Gingery Bread

**Servings:** 10 **Yield:** 10 servings

## Ingredients

- 3 cups all-purpose flour
- 1 tablespoon ground cinnamon
- 2 teaspoons baking soda
- 1 ½ teaspoons ground cloves
- 1 teaspoon ground ginger
- ¾ teaspoon salt
- 1 ½ cups white sugar
- 1 cup vegetable oil
- 1 cup dark molasses
- ½ cup apple juice
- 2 large eggs eggs
- 1 tablespoon grated fresh ginger
- ½ cup chopped crystallized ginger

## Directions

### Step 1

Preheat oven to 350 degrees F (175 degrees C). Butter and flour a 10 inch springform pan.

### Step 2

Stir together flour, cinnamon, cloves, ground ginger, baking soda, and salt.

### Step 3

In a large bowl, mix sugar with oil, juice, molasses, eggs, and fresh ginger in a large bowl. Mix in crystallized ginger. Stir in flour mixture. Pour into prepared pan.

### Step 4

Bake for 1 hour, or until cake tester comes out clean. Run a knife around the edge to loosen cake, and release pan sides. Serve warm.

## Nutrition Facts

### Per Serving:

581.4 calories; protein 5.2g 11% DV; carbohydrates 89.5g 29% DV; fat 23.5g 36% DV; cholesterol 37.2mg 12% DV; sodium 457mg 18% DV.

# Billy Pudding for Davey

**Prep:** 15 mins **Cook:** 1 hr **Additional:** 8 hrs **Total:** 9 hrs 15 mins **Servings:** 10 **Yield:** 10 servings

## Ingredients

- 1 cup pearl tapioca
- 5 ½ cups water
- 3 cups brown sugar
- 1 cup chopped dates
- 1 cup chopped walnuts
- 2 tablespoons butter, melted
- 1 pinch ground cinnamon
- 1 pinch salt

## Directions

### Step 1

Stir the tapioca into the water in a bowl, and allow to soak 8 hours or overnight.

### Step 2

Preheat oven to 300 degrees F (150 degrees C). Grease a 2-quart baking dish.

### Step 3

Mix the soaked tapioca, brown sugar, dates, walnuts, butter, cinnamon, and salt together in a large bowl; transfer to the prepared baking dish.

### Step 4

Bake until set, about 1 hour. Serve warm.

## Nutrition Facts

**Per Serving:**

359.3 calories; protein 2.4g 5% DV; carbohydrates 69.3g 22% DV; fat 10g 15% DV; cholesterol 6.1mg 2% DV; sodium 33.6mg 1% DV.

# Ice Box Fruit Cake

**Prep:** 15 mins **Additional:** 1 day **Total:** 1 day **Servings:** 12 **Yield:** 12 servings

## Ingredients

- 1 pound chopped pecans
- 1 (15 ounce) package raisins
- 1 (14 ounce) package sweetened flaked coconut

- 1 (13.5 ounce) package graham cracker crumbs
- 1 (4 ounce) jar maraschino cherries, drained and chopped
- 1 (14 ounce) can low-fat sweetened condensed milk (such as Eagle Brand)

**Directions**

**Step 1**

Line a 9x9-inch dish or decorative container with waxed paper.

**Step 2**

Mix pecans, raisins, coconut, graham cracker crumbs, and cherries together in a bowl using your hands; stir in sweetened condensed milk. Press mixture into the prepared dish. Cover dish with plastic wrap or a tight-fitting lid. Refrigerate for 1 day.

**Nutrition Facts**

**Per Serving:**

811.2 calories; protein 11.3g 23% DV; carbohydrates 103.7g 34% DV; fat 41.5g 64% DV; cholesterol 5.8mg 2% DV; sodium 334.4mg 13% DV.

# Chocolate-Almond Cheesecake

**Prep:** 15 mins **Cook:** 45 mins **Additional:** 5 hrs **Total:** 6 hrs **Servings:** 16 **Yield:** 16 servings, 1 piece (80 g) each

**Ingredients**

- 1 (200 g) package almond-flavoured cookies (Amaretti), finely crushed
- ¼ cup butter, melted
- 1 cup chocolate-covered almonds, chopped, divided
- 3 (250 g) packages PHILADELPHIA Chocolate Brick Cream Cheese, softened
- ¾ cup sugar
- 3 large eggs eggs

**Directions**

**Step 1**

Heat oven to 350 degrees F (175 degrees C).

**Step 2**

Mix cookie crumbs and butter; press onto bottom of 9-inch springform pan. Sprinkle with 1/2 cup nuts.

**Step 3**

Beat cream cheese and sugar in large bowl with mixer until blended. Add eggs, 1 at a time, mixing on low speed after each just until blended; pour over crust.

**Step 4**

Bake 40 to 45 minutes or until centre is almost set. Run knife around rim of pan to loosen cake; cool before removing rim. Refrigerate cheesecake 4 hours. Top with remaining nuts before serving.

**Nutrition Facts**

**Per Serving:**

365.9 calories; protein 6.2g 12% DV; carbohydrates 35.3g 11% DV; fat 23g 35% DV; cholesterol 86.5mg 29% DV; sodium 192.2mg 8% DV.

# Fermented Fruit Cake Wrap

**Prep:** 10 mins **Additional:** 1 week 3 days **Total:** 1 week 3 days **Servings:** 10 **Yield:** 1 fruitcake

**Ingredients**

- 1 cup grapefruit juice, or to taste
- 1 (1 pound) baked and cooled fruitcake
- 1 cheesecloth

**Directions**

**Step 1**

Pour grapefruit juice into a large bowl and add cheesecloth; allow to soak. Wrap the cake in the grapefruit-soaked cheesecloth; wrap again in 2 layers of aluminum foil. Store in a cool place for up to 2 or 3 months.

**Nutrition Facts**

**Per Serving:**

156.6 calories; protein 1.4g 3% DV; carbohydrates 30.2g 10% DV; fat 4.2g 6% DV; cholesterol 2.3mg 1% DV; sodium 122.7mg 5% DV.

# Yukon Cornelius Pull-Apart Cupcake Cake

**Prep:** 1 hr 30 mins **Cook:** 25 mins **Additional:** 1 hr 25 mins **Total:** 3 hrs 20 mins **Servings:** 24 **Yield:** 24 cupcakes

## Ingredients

### Cupcakes:

- 1 ¾ cups all-purpose flour
- 1 cup dark cocoa powder (such as Hershey's Special Dark), sifted
- 2 teaspoons baking soda
- 1 teaspoon baking powder
- ¾ teaspoon salt
- 1 cup firmly packed brown sugar
- ½ cup white sugar
- ½ cup unsalted butter, softened
- 2 large eggs, at room temperature
- 2 teaspoons vanilla extract
- 1 cup strongly brewed coffee, cooled to room temperature
- 1 cup sour cream

### Peppermint-White Chocolate Ganache:

- 20 ounces white chocolate chips (such as Ghirardelli)
- 8 ounces heavy cream
- ⅓ cup crushed peppermint candies
- ½ teaspoon peppermint extract, or to taste

### Peppermint Buttercream Frosting:

- 1 ½ cups unsalted butter, softened
- 5 cups powdered sugar, or as needed
- 1 ½ teaspoons vanilla extract
- 1 teaspoon peppermint extract, or to taste
- ¼ teaspoon salt
- ⅓ cup heavy cream, or as needed

### For Decorating:

- 6 drops yellow food coloring, or as needed, divided
- 1 teaspoon cocoa powder, or as needed
- 6 drops red food coloring, or as needed, divided
- 1 (10.5 ounce) package large marshmallows
- 1 (12 ounce) bag dark chocolate chips
- piping bags
- couplers
- large round piping tips
- large open star piping tip

## Directions

### Step 1

Preheat the oven to 350 degrees F (175 degrees C). Line two 12-cup standard cupcake pans with paper liners.

**Step 2**

Whisk flour, cocoa powder, baking soda, baking powder, and salt together in a medium bowl.

**Step 3**

Combine sugars and butter in a large bowl; beat with an electric mixer until light and fluffy. Beat in eggs one at a time, thoroughly mixing after each addition. Beat in vanilla extract.

**Step 4**

Mix 1/3 of the flour mixture into the butter mixture until just combined. Mix in 1/2 of the coffee and 1/2 of the sour cream until just combined. Add remaining flour mixture alternately with remaining sour cream and coffee. Do not overmix. Fill the prepared cupcake cups evenly with batter.

**Step 5**

Bake in the preheated oven until they spring back lightly when touched, 18 to 22 minutes. Let cool completely, 30 minutes to 1 hour.

**Step 6**

Core cooled cupcakes using a knife or cupcake corer, cutting about halfway down. Save cupcake centers for another use (such as for making a batch of cake balls).

**Step 7**

Prepare ganache. Add white chocolate chips and heavy cream to a large, microwave-safe bowl. Heat at 50% power until chocolate is melted and smooth, in 30-second intervals, stirring after each. Mix in crushed candies and peppermint extract until thoroughly combined. Allow to cool for 10 minutes, stirring often.

**Step 8**

Place ganache in a piping bag or resealable plastic bag with a corner cut off. Fill each cupcake to the top with ganache. Allow them to sit until ganache firms up and doesn't "smudge" when pressed lightly with fingertips, 15 to 20 minutes.

**Step 9**

Prepare frosting. Cream butter until smooth in a large bowl with an electric mixer. Beat in 1 cup powdered sugar at a time, mixing well after each addition. Mix in vanilla extract, peppermint extract, and salt. Add heavy cream and beat on medium-high speed until light and fluffy, 3 to 5 minutes. If frosting is too thick, add more heavy cream--or if it is too thin, add more powdered sugar until frosting is a spreadable consistency that still holds its shape.

**Step 10**

Place a small amount of frosting in a separate bowl and add yellow food coloring for the ear muffs. Divide remaining frosting in half. To 1/2 of the divided frosting, add cocoa powder and red food coloring to achieve an auburn color. Divide remaining white frosting in half again. Color 1/2 peach using a very light amount of red and yellow food coloring. Color remaining frosting red. Put each into a piping bag fitted with a coupler.

## Step 11

Arrange cupcakes on a large cake board or serving platter, starting from the top. Begin with 1 cupcake at the top. Follow with a row of 2 cupcakes, making sure they stay as close as possible. (If cupcakes slide around, affix a small amount of frosting to the bottom of them so they stick to the serving platter or cake board.) Follow with a row of 3 cupcakes, then a row of 5 cupcakes, a row of 4 cupcakes, another row of 5 cupcakes, and finally a last row of 4 cupcakes. Make sure the cupcakes are as close to one another as possible. If there are any large gaps, you can use large marshmallows, trimmed to fit, in order to fill them in and make a flatter, more cohesive surface to frost.

## Step 12

Beginning with the top 6 cupcakes (the rows with 1 cupcake, 2 cupcakes, and 3 cupcakes in them), frost the hat portion of the cake using the red frosting and large round tip. Smooth center portion using an offset spatula, if desired. Use the peach frosting to frost the center 3 cupcakes in the row of 5 below the hat, leaving a cupcake on each side unfrosted for the ear muffs. Smooth with an offset spatula. Affix 2 dark chocolate chips upside-down for the eyes in the center of the peach frosting.

## Step 13

Pipe the nose below the eyes, and then the lower lip below the nose using the peach frosting. Frost the cupcakes on each side of the face with the yellow frosting for the ear muffs. To frost the beard, use the auburn colored frosting and cover the remaining unfrosted cupcakes (that contain a row of 4, a row of 5, and final row of 4 cupcakes) with a thin layer of the auburn frosting. Smooth frosting all over the "beard-portion" of the cupcakes until mostly smooth and flat. Place a star tip on the auburn frosting piping bag, and pipe dots of frosting along the side of the face, then pipe the mustache between the nose and lip, and add some swirls on top of the beard, if desired.

## Step 14

Allow cupcake cake to sit for about 30 minutes at room temperature (or place in the fridge) to allow frosting to crust. Serve.

### Nutrition Facts

### Per Serving:

653.4 calories; protein 5.5g 11% DV; carbohydrates 85g 27% DV; fat 35.1g 54% DV; cholesterol 82.8mg 28% DV; sodium 283.5mg 11% DV.

# Christmas Chocolate Town Cake

**Prep:** 20 mins **Cook:** 40 mins **Total:** 1 hr **Servings:** 12 **Yield:** 2 - 9 inch round pans

## Ingredients

- ½ cup unsweetened cocoa powder
- ½ cup boiling water
- ⅔ cup shortening
- 1 ¾ cups white sugar
- 1 teaspoon vanilla extract
- 2 large eggs eggs
- 2 ½ cups all-purpose flour
- 1 teaspoon baking soda
- 1 teaspoon salt
- 1 ⅓ cups buttermilk

## Directions

### Step 1

Preheat oven to 350 degrees F (175 degrees C). Grease and flour 2 - 9 inch pans. Sift together the flour, baking soda and salt. Set aside.

### Step 2

Combine cocoa and boiling water in small bowl to form a smooth paste. Cool slightly.

### Step 3

In a large bowl, cream together the shortening, sugar and vanilla until light and fluffy. Beat in the eggs one at a time. Beat in the flour mixture alternately with the buttermilk, mixing just until incorporated. Blend in cocoa paste.

### Step 4

Divide batter into 2 prepared 9 inch pans. Bake in the preheated oven for 35 to 40 minutes, or until a toothpick inserted into the center of the cake comes out clean. Cool 10 minutes in pans then turn out onto wire rack and cool completely.

## Nutrition Facts

### Per Serving:

342.2 calories; protein 5.3g 11% DV; carbohydrates 52.4g 17% DV; fat 13.2g 20% DV; cholesterol 38.5mg 13% DV; sodium 340.2mg 14% DV.

# Santa Leg Cupcakes

**Prep:** 45 mins **Total:** 45 mins **Servings:** 12 **Yield:** 12 cupcakes

## Ingredients

- 12 eaches unfrosted cupcakes, cooled
- 1 (16 ounce) package vanilla frosting
- 10 ounces red fondant
- 3 ounces black fondant
- 3 ounces white fondant

## Directions

### Step 1

Spread a thick layer of white frosting onto each cupcake. Create a snow-like effect with a palette knife or the back of a spoon.

### Step 2

Spoon the remaining frosting into a piping bag with a small round tip. Pipe rows of rectangles, offset from one another, onto the base of the cupcake to create 'bricks'.

### Step 3

Shape red fondant into 24 small cylinders for Santa's legs. Shape the black fondant into 24 boots or shoes. Divide the white fondant into 24 balls and flatten into round circles.

### Step 4

Glue the white fondant circles onto the bottom of each red leg with a bit of water. Affix a black boot to the bottom of each red leg, then use a spoon to create the soles.

### Step 5

Use your fingers to slightly narrow the other end of each leg. Stick the narrow ends of two legs into each cupcake. Repeat with remaining legs and cupcakes.

## Nutrition Facts

### Per Serving:

434.9 calories; protein 1.8g 4% DV; carbohydrates 76.6g 25% DV; fat 13.4g 21% DV; cholesterol 18.4mg 6% DV; sodium 187.5mg 8% DV.

# Moon Rocks

**Prep:** 20 mins **Cook:** 20 mins **Total:** 40 mins **Servings:** 24 **Yield:** 2 dozen

## Ingredients

- 1 cup semisweet chocolate chips
- 2 cups all-purpose flour
- 1 ½ teaspoons baking soda
- ½ teaspoon salt
- ½ cup butter, softened

- 1 ½ cups packed light brown sugar
- 3 large eggs eggs
- 1 teaspoon vanilla extract
- 1 cup water
- 2 cups miniature marshmallows

## Directions

### Step 1

Preheat oven to 350 degrees F (175 degrees C).

### Step 2

Melt chocolate in the top of a double boiler. Let cool.

### Step 3

In a mixing bowl, combine flour, baking soda and salt. In a separate bowl, cream butter and sugar together. Blend eggs into the butter mixture one at a time. Stir the vanilla, flour mixture, water and chocolate into the butter and eggs; beat well. Stir in marshmallows. Fill paper-lined cupcake pans half full.

### Step 4

Bake in a preheated 350 degrees F (175 degrees C) oven for 20 minutes. Cool on a wire rack before serving.

## Nutrition Facts

## Per Serving:

181.1 calories; protein 2.3g 5% DV; carbohydrates 29.3g 10% DV; fat 6.7g 10% DV; cholesterol 36.7mg 12% DV; sodium 170.3mg 7% DV.

# Cranberry Cheesecake Bars

**Prep:** 15 mins **Cook:** 35 mins **Total:** 50 mins **Servings:** 16 **Yield:** 1 9x13-inch pan

## Ingredients

### Crust:

- 1 (18.25 ounce) package butter cake mix
- ½ cup butter, softened
- 1 egg
- ¼ cup chopped pecans

### Filling:

- 1 (8 ounce) package cream cheese, softened
- ¼ cup confectioners' sugar
- 1 egg
- ½ teaspoon vanilla extract
- 1 (16 ounce) can whole berry cranberry sauce
- ¼ teaspoon ground nutmeg

## Directions

### Step 1

Preheat oven to 350 degrees F (175 degrees C).

### Step 2

Beat cake mix, butter, and 1 egg together in a bowl using an electric mixer on low speed until mixture is crumbly; stir in pecans. Press mixture into a 9x13-inch baking dish.

### Step 3

Bake in the preheated oven until crust is set, 5 to 8 minutes.

### Step 4

Beat cream cheese, confectioners' sugar, 1 egg, and vanilla extract together in a bowl using an electric mixer until smooth. Stir cranberry sauce and nutmeg together in a separate bowl. Carefully spread cream cheese mixture onto crust. Spoon cranberry sauce mixture in 3 rows lengthwise over cream cheese mixture. Pull a knife through cranberry sauce mixture into cream cheese mixture to form swirls.

### Step 5

Bake in the preheated oven until cream cheese mixture is set, 30 to 40 minutes. Cool completely before cutting into bars.

**Nutrition Facts**

**Per Serving:**

294.1 calories; protein 2.8g 6% DV; carbohydrates 39g 13% DV; fat 14.7g 23% DV; cholesterol 52.5mg 18% DV; sodium 297.1mg 12% DV.

# Sago Plum Pudding

**Prep:** 5 hrs 15 mins **Cook:** 4 hrs **Additional:** 3 hrs **Total:** 12 hrs 15 mins **Servings:** 8 **Yield:** 8 servings

## Ingredients

- 2 ¼ ounces pearl sago
- 1 cup milk
- 1 teaspoon baking soda
- ⅝ cup dark brown sugar
- 2 cups fresh bread crumbs
- ½ cup golden raisins
- ½ cup dried currants
- ½ cup chopped dates
- 2 large eggs eggs, lightly beaten
- ¼ cup butter, melted

## Directions

### Step 1

In a small bowl, combine sago and milk; cover and refrigerate 8 hours or overnight.

### Step 2

Grease a 6 cup pudding basin.

### Step 3

In a large bowl, stir together sago mixture and baking soda until soda is dissolved. Stir in brown sugar, bread crumbs, raisins, currants, dates, eggs and butter until well combined. Spoon into prepared basin. Place a piece of waxed or parchment paper over the top of the basin and secure the lid.

### Step 4

Place the basin on a trivet or dish in a large pot and fill the pot with boiling water to come halfway up the sides of the basin. Bring the water to a boil again, then reduce the heat, cover and simmer 3 1/2 to 4 hours, topping off water as necessary, until pudding is firm.

## Nutrition Facts

**Per Serving:**

290.2 calories; protein 4.6g 9% DV; carbohydrates 52.7g 17% DV; fat 8.1g 12% DV; cholesterol 64.2mg 21% DV; sodium 312.4mg 13% DV.

# Carrot-Oatmeal Spice Cake

**Servings:** 15 **Yield:** 1 - 7x11 inch pan

## Ingredients

- 1 cup raisins
- ⅓ cup shredded carrots
- 2 cups water
- 1 cup all-purpose flour
- 1 cup quick cooking oats
- 1 ½ teaspoons artificial sweetener
- ½ teaspoon salt
- 1 teaspoon baking soda
- 1 teaspoon ground cinnamon
- ½ cup margarine, softened
- ¼ cup egg substitute
- 1 teaspoon vanilla extract
- ⅓ cup pecans, coarsely chopped

## Directions

### Step 1

Preheat oven to 350 degrees F (175 degrees C). Grease a 7x11 inch baking dish. Set aside.

### Step 2

Combine raisins, carrots, and water in a medium saucepan. Bring to a boil, reduce heat and simmer for 10 minutes. Remove from heat and allow to cool.

### Step 3

In a mixing bowl, combine flour, oatmeal, sugar substitute, salt, baking soda and cinnamon.

### Step 4

In a separate bowl, mix together the margarine, egg substitute, and vanilla. Add to the flour mixture and mix well.

### Step 5

Add the raisin mixture and nuts, mix well and pour into baking pan.

### Step 6

Bake for 35 minutes or until toothpick inserted in middle comes out clean.

## Nutrition Facts

### Per Serving:

157.5 calories; protein 3.2g 6% DV; carbohydrates 18.5g 6% DV; fat 8.3g 13% DV; cholesterolmg; sodium 242.3mg 10% DV.

# Red and Green Velvet Cake!

**Prep:** 15 mins **Cook:** 25 mins **Additional:** 30 mins **Total:** 1 hr 10 mins **Servings:** 12 **Yield:** 1 9x12-inch sheet cake

## Ingredients

- ½ cup vegetable shortening
- 1 ½ cups white sugar
- 2 large eggs eggs
- 1 cup buttermilk
- 2 tablespoons unsweetened cocoa powder
- 1 teaspoon salt
- 1 teaspoon vanilla extract
- 2 ½ cups sifted all-purpose flour

- 2 tablespoons red food coloring, or as needed
- 2 tablespoons green food coloring, or as needed
- ¾ teaspoon baking soda
- 1 ½ teaspoons distilled white vinegar
- ¾ teaspoon baking soda
- 1 ½ teaspoons distilled white vinegar

## Directions

### Step 1

Preheat oven to 350 degrees F (175 degrees C).

### Step 2

Grease a 9x13-inch sheet pan.

### Step 3

Mash vegetable shortening and sugar together in a large bowl until smooth and creamy; beat in eggs until fully incorporated.

### Step 4

Stir buttermilk, cocoa powder, salt, and vanilla extract into the shortening mixture until the liquid ingredients are an even color and texture.

### Step 5

Sift flour into the liquid ingredients until combined.

### Step 6

Pour half the batter into a separate bowl.

### Step 7

Lightly stir red food color into one bowl of batter and green food color into the other bowl of batter.

### Step 8

Quickly fold 3/4 teaspoon baking soda and 1 1/2 teaspoon white vinegar into the bowl of red batter; quickly fold 3/4 teaspoon baking soda and 1 1/2 teaspoon white vinegar into the bowl of green batter.

### Step 9

Pour the red and green batters into the prepared sheet pan in alternating colors.

### Step 10

Bake in the preheated oven until the cake is lightly browned on top and a toothpick inserted in the center comes out clean, 25 to 30 minutes. Allow to cool completely before frosting.

### Cook's Note:

I prefer to ice this cake with a buttercream icing, sometimes simple white icing if I don't have the buttercream on me. If you're using two 9-inch round pans, you could easily make one layer red and one layer green instead of alternating the colors in both layers.

### Nutrition Facts

### Per Serving:

290.3 calories; protein 4.6g 9% DV; carbohydrates 46.4g 15% DV; fat 9.9g 15% DV; cholesterol 31.8mg 11% DV; sodium 385mg 15% DV.

# Virginia Whiskey Cake

**Prep:** 20 mins **Cook:** 1 hr **Total:** 1 hr 20 mins **Servings:** 12 **Yield:** 1 loaf

### Ingredients

- ¼ cup butter, softened
- ¼ cup white sugar
- 3 eaches egg yolks
- 1 ½ cups all-purpose flour
- 1 teaspoon baking powder
- ¼ teaspoon ground nutmeg
- ½ cup port wine
- ⅛ cup brandy
- ¾ cup candied mixed fruit
- 3 large egg whites egg whites
- ½ cup bourbon whiskey

### Directions

### Step 1

Preheat the oven to 325 degrees F (165 degrees C). Grease an 9x5 inch loaf pan.

### Step 2

In a medium bowl, cream together the butter and sugar until light and fluffy. Gradually beat in the egg yolks until well blended. Combine the flour, baking powder, and nutmeg; stir into the batter alternately with the port wine and brandy. Fold in the candied fruit.

**Step 3**

In a separate clean dry bowl, whip egg whites to soft peaks. Fold 1/4 of the egg whites into the batter to lighten, then fold in the remaining whites. Pour into the prepared loaf pan.

**Step 4**

Bake for 1 hour in the preheated oven, or until a toothpick inserted into the center of the loaf comes out clean. Cool cake in the pan, and pour the bourbon over it. When the bourbon has soaked in, remove it from the pan, and wrap with aluminum foil. Let it sit for at least 1 day before serving.

**Nutrition Facts**

**Per Serving:**

211.6 calories; protein 3.3g 7% DV; carbohydrates 28.7g 9% DV; fat 5.2g 8% DV; cholesterol 61.4mg 21% DV; sodium 117.5mg 5% DV.

# Japanese Fruit Cake

**Prep:** 50 mins **Cook:** 25 mins **Total:** 1 hr 15 mins **Servings:** 12 **Yield:** 1 - 9 inch 3 layer cake

**Ingredients**

- 1 cup butter
- 2 cups white sugar
- 4 large eggs eggs
- 1 teaspoon vanilla extract
- 3 cups all-purpose flour
- 3 teaspoons baking powder
- ½ teaspoon salt
- ½ cup milk
- 1 teaspoon ground cloves
- 1 teaspoon ground cinnamon
- 1 teaspoon ground allspice

- 1 ½ cups chopped raisins
- ¾ cup chopped almonds
- 4 tablespoons grated orange zest
- 1 cup fresh orange juice
- 4 cups flaked coconut
- 2 cups white sugar
- 1 cup boiling water
- 1 teaspoon cornstarch
- 1 recipe seven minute frosting (from recipe link)

**Directions**

**Step 1**

Preheat oven to 325 degrees F (165 degrees C). Grease and flour three 9 inch round cake pans.

## Step 2

Cream together butter, 2 cups sugar, eggs, and vanilla.

## Step 3

Sift together flour, baking powder, and salt. Add flour mixture alternately with milk into egg mixture. Divide batter into 3 parts. Fill two pans with plain batter. Add spices, raisins, and nuts into remaining batter, and pour batter into third pan.

## Step 4

Bake for 25 minutes, or until done. Cool layers on wire racks.

## Step 5

Mix together orange juice and rind, 2 cups coconut, 2 cups sugar, boiling water, and cornstarch in a 2 quart pan. Bring to a boil, and cook until mixture falls in lumps from a spoon. Put layers together with filling, placing spiced layer in the center. Ice cake with Seven Minute Frosting, and cover with remaining coconut.

**Nutrition Facts**

**Per Serving:**

953.1 calories; protein 10g 20% DV; carbohydrates 143.5g 46% DV; fat 40.8g 63% DV; cholesterol 103.7mg 35% DV; sodium 379.3mg 15% DV.

# Candy Popcorn Cake

**Servings:** 16 **Yield:** 1 bundt cake

## Ingredients

- 1 cup butter
- 32 regulars large marshmallows
- 16 cups popped popcorn
- 1 cup gumdrops, no black ones
- 1 cup chocolate covered peanuts
- 1 cup candy-coated milk chocolate pieces

## Directions

## Step 1

Melt the butter and marshmallows in heavy pan over low heat. Stir often.

## Step 2

Put popcorn in a large bowl and pour marshmallow mix over top. Stir well to mix. Add the candy and nuts, and mix together. Pack into a greased 12-cup bundt pan. Let set till cooled. Turn out onto a plate to serve. Cut in wedges.

**Nutrition Facts**

**Per Serving:**

358.7 calories; protein 3.2g 6% DV; carbohydrates 43.1g 14% DV; fat 20.5g 32% DV; cholesterol 33.2mg 11% DV; sodium 207.2mg 8% DV.

# Buche de Noel (Yule Log)

**Prep:** 45 mins **Cook:** 11 mins **Additional:** 38 mins **Total:** 1 hr 34 mins **Servings:** 10 **Yield:** 1 log

**Ingredients**

**Cake:**

- 2 teaspoons butter
- ⅓ cup all-purpose flour, sifted
- ⅓ cup unsweetened cocoa powder
- ¼ teaspoon fine salt

- 4 large eggs eggs, separated
- ¾ cup confectioners' sugar, divided
- 1 teaspoon vanilla extract

**Whipped Cream Filling:**

- 1 cup heavy whipping cream
- 3 tablespoons confectioners' sugar
- 1 tablespoon sour cream

- Chocolate Ganache:
- ½ cup heavy whipping cream
- 8 ounces dark chocolate chips

**Directions**

**Step 1**

Preheat oven to 350 degrees F (175 degrees C). Grease a 9x13-inch jelly roll pan with 1 teaspoon butter and line with parchment paper. Grease parchment paper with 1 teaspoon butter.

**Step 2**

Whisk flour, cocoa powder, and salt together in a small bowl.

**Step 3**

Combine egg yolks, 1/4 cup confectioners' sugar, and vanilla extract in a bowl; beat with an electric mixer on medium-high speed until pale yellow, 3 to 4 minutes.

**Step 4**

Clean the beaters of the electric mixer. Beat egg whites in a bowl on medium-high speed until foamy, 1 to 2 minutes. Gradually add 1/2 cup confectioners' sugar and beat until stiff peaks form, 2 to 3 minutes more.

**Step 5**

Fold egg yolk mixture gently into the egg whites. Fold flour mixture in gradually until batter is smooth.

**Step 6**

Pour batter into the prepared jelly roll pan and spread evenly with an offset spatula.

**Step 7**

Bake in the preheated oven until a toothpick inserted into the center comes out clean, 8 to 10 minutes. Let cool, about 30 minutes.

**Step 8**

Combine 1 cup heavy cream, 3 tablespoons confectioners' sugar, and sour cream in a bowl; blend with an electric mixer on medium-high speed until stiff, 1 to 2 minutes.

**Step 9**

Turn the jelly roll pan so the shorter side faces you. Spread whipped cream over the cake, leaving a 2-inch border at the top. Roll up cake toward the uncovered border, letting the parchment paper fall away as you roll. Place roll seam-side down on a serving platter.

**Step 10**

Place 1/2 cup heavy cream in a small saucepan over medium-low heat until warmed through, 3 to 5 minutes. Remove from heat and stir in chocolate chips. Let stand until chocolate softens, about 3 minutes. Stir with a spatula or wooden spoon until ganache is smooth and creamy.

**Step 11**

Drizzle chocolate ganache over rolled cake. Let stand until set, about 5 minutes. Run a fork through the ganache to create a tree bark effect.

**Nutrition Facts**

**Per Serving:**

336.8 calories; protein 5.4g 11% DV; carbohydrates 32.8g 11% DV; fat 22.7g 35% DV; cholesterol 126.1mg 42% DV; sodium 113mg 5% DV.

# Grasshopper Cheesecake Bars

**Prep:** 15 mins **Cook:** 35 mins **Total:** 50 mins **Servings:** 25 **Yield:** 25 bars

## Ingredients

### Crust:

- ¾ cup all-purpose flour
- ⅓ cup white sugar
- ⅓ cup unsweetened cocoa powder
- 6 tablespoons cold butter

### Filling:

- 1 (8 ounce) package cream cheese, at room temperature
- ¼ cup white sugar
- 1 egg
- 1 teaspoon peppermint extract
- 5 drops green food coloring
- ¼ cup milk

## Directions

### Step 1

Preheat the oven to 350 degrees F (175 degrees C).

### Step 2

Mix flour, sugar, and cocoa powder in a large bowl. Cut in butter until mixture resembles fine crumbs. Set aside 1 cup of the crumbs to be used as the topping. Press remaining crumb mixture into an ungreased 8x8-inch baking pan.

### Step 3

Bake crust in the preheated oven until set, about 15 minutes. Remove and let cool. Keep oven on.

### Step 4

While crust is cooling, beat cream cheese and sugar with an electric mixer until fluffy. Add egg, peppermint extract, and green food coloring; beat well. Stir in milk until batter is smooth. Pour batter over the cooled crust. Sprinkle reserved crumb mixture on top.

### Step 5

Bake until filling is set, 20 to 25 minutes. Cool before cutting into 25 bars.

## Nutrition Facts

## Per Serving:

94.5 calories; protein 1.6g 3% DV; carbohydrates 8.5g 3% DV; fat 6.3g 10% DV; cholesterol 24.8mg 8% DV; sodium 50.3mg 2% DV.

# Christmas Eggnog Cheesecake

**Prep:** 45 mins **Cook:** 1 hr 5 mins **Additional:** 3 hrs 30 mins **Total:** 5 hrs 20 mins **Servings:** 12 **Yield:** 1 9-inch cheesecake

## Ingredients

### Crust:

- 8 large rectangular piece or 2 squares or 4 small rectangular pieces whole graham crackers
- 1 teaspoon white sugar
- ¼ teaspoon ground ginger
- ¼ teaspoon ground nutmeg
- ¼ teaspoon ground cinnamon
- ¼ cup butter, melted

### Filling:

- 4 (8 ounce) packages cream cheese, room temperature
- ¾ cup white sugar
- ¼ cup all-purpose flour
- ¼ teaspoon ground nutmeg
- ¼ teaspoon ground cinnamon
- 1 pinch ground cloves
- 1 egg
- 1 ¾ cups prepared eggnog
- 1 teaspoon vanilla extract
- 1 (8 ounce) carton sour cream
- 1 pinch ground nutmeg, or more to taste

## Directions

### Step 1

Preheat oven to 350 degrees F (175 degrees C).

### Step 2

Process graham crackers in a food processor to make crumbs; pulse 1 teaspoon sugar, ginger, 1/4 teaspoon nutmeg, and 1/4 teaspoon cinnamon with crumbs once or twice to combine. With processor running, drizzle butter into crumbs just to incorporate. Press graham cracker mixture into the bottom of a 9-inch spring form pan.

### Step 3

Bake crust in the preheated oven for 10 minutes; cool on wire rack.

### Step 4

Beat cream cheese in a large bowl with an electric mixer on medium speed until smooth. Stir 3/4 cup sugar, flour, 1/4 teaspoon nutmeg, 1/4 teaspoon cinnamon, and cloves in a bowl. Beat sugar mixture into cream cheese until smooth; beat in egg. Slowly beat eggnog into cream cheese mixture, followed by vanilla extract. Pour cream cheese filling into spring form pan over the crust. Tap pan lightly on a work surface to release air bubbles.

### Step 5

Bake in the oven for 1 hour.

### Step 6

Spread sour cream over filling. Return to oven and bake 5 more minutes.

### Step 7

Cool in pan on a rack until cool to the touch, about 30 minutes, before refrigerating to chill thoroughly. Sprinkle with ground nutmeg to taste before serving.

**Nutrition Facts**

**Per Serving:**

492.4 calories; protein 9.1g 18% DV; carbohydrates 30.1g 10% DV; fat 38.1g 59% DV; cholesterol 138mg 46% DV; sodium 340.9mg 14% DV.

# Ghirardelli Mini Gingerbread-Chocolate Chip Cupcakes With Molasses Buttercream

**Prep:** 30 mins **Cook:** 15 mins **Additional:** 45 mins **Total:** 1 hr 30 mins **Servings:** 48 **Yield:** 4 dozen

**Ingredients**

**Cupcakes:**

- 2 ½ cups all-purpose flour
- ⅓ cup chopped crystallized ginger
- ¾ teaspoon baking soda
- ½ teaspoon table salt
- ½ teaspoon ground cinnamon
- ⅛ teaspoon ground cloves
- ¼ cup unsalted butter, softened
- ¼ cup granulated sugar
- ¼ cup packed light brown sugar

- ½ cup unsweetened applesauce
- 2 large eggs
- 1 cup hot strongly brewed coffee
- ⅓ cup unsulfured molasses
- 1 cup Ghirardelli Semi-Sweet Chocolate Baking Chips
- 48 miniature paper baking cups
- Cooking spray

**Molasses Buttercream:**

- ¾ cup unsalted butter, softened

- 1 ½ tablespoons unsulfured molasses

- ⅛ teaspoon table salt
- 4 ½ cups powdered sugar
- 3 tablespoons whole milk, or more as needed

**Chocolate Trees:**

- 1 cup Ghirardelli Semi-Sweet Chocolate Baking Chips

**Garnish:**

- Finely chopped crystallized ginger

## Directions

### Step 1

Prepare the Cupcakes: Preheat oven to 350 degrees F. Place flour, crystallized ginger, baking soda, salt, cinnamon, and cloves in a food processor; process until ginger is finely ground, about 1 minute.

### Step 2

Beat butter, granulated sugar, and brown sugar with a heavy-duty stand mixer fitted with paddle attachment on medium speed until light and fluffy, 2 to 3 minutes. Beat in applesauce until blended. Add eggs one at a time, beating just until blended after each addition.

### Step 3

Stir together hot brewed coffee and molasses in a 2-cup glass measuring cup until blended. Add flour mixture to butter mixture alternately with coffee mixture, beginning and ending with flour mixture. Beat on low speed just until blended after each addition. Gently stir in Ghirardelli Semi-Sweet Chocolate Baking Chips.

### Step 4

Place 48 miniature paper baking cups in four 12-cup miniature muffin pans, and coat cups with cooking spray. Spoon batter into cups, filling almost full.

### Step 5

Bake in preheated oven until a wooden pick inserted in center comes out clean, 12 to 14 minutes. Remove from pan to a wire rack and cool completely, about 30 minutes.

### Step 6

Prepare the Molasses Buttercream: Beat butter in a large bowl with an electric mixer on medium speed until smooth; beat in molasses and salt until fully incorporated, about 1 minute. Gradually add powdered sugar and 3 tablespoons of the milk; beat until light and fluffy, about 2 minutes. If needed, add remaining 1 tablespoon milk, 1 teaspoon at a time, and beat until desired consistency is reached.

### Step 7

Prepare the Chocolate Trees: Place 1 cup Ghirardelli Semi-Sweet Chocolate Baking Chips in a small microwaveable bowl, and microwave on medium (50% power) until melted and smooth, 1 to 2 minutes, stirring every 30 seconds. Transfer mixture to a piping bag or heavy-duty zip-top bag with a very small hole snipped in the corner.

## Step 8

Pipe into small Christmas tree shapes on a parchment paper-lined baking sheet. Chill until set, about 15 minutes; keep chilled until ready to use.

## Step 9

Pipe or dollop Molasses Buttercream on cupcakes. Garnish with finely chopped crystallized ginger, and top with chocolate Christmas trees.

## Nutrition Facts

## Per Serving:

159.9 calories; protein 1.5g 3% DV; carbohydrates 26.8g 9% DV; fat 6.2g 10% DV; cholesterol 17.9mg 6% DV; sodium 55.8mg 2% DV.

# Gumdrop Fruitcake

**Servings:** 28 **Yield:** 1 - 10 inch tube pan

## Ingredients

- 1 cup butter
- 2 cups white sugar
- 2 large eggs eggs, beaten
- 4 cups all-purpose flour
- 1 teaspoon ground cinnamon
- ¼ teaspoon ground cloves
- ¼ teaspoon ground nutmeg
- ¼ teaspoon salt

- 1 ½ cups applesauce
- 1 teaspoon baking soda
- 1 tablespoon hot water
- 1 teaspoon vanilla extract
- 16 ounces gumdrops, no black ones
- 3 cups raisins
- 1 cup chopped pecans
- 1 tablespoon butter

## Directions

## Step 1

Preheat oven to 325 degrees F (165 degrees C). Line two 9 x 5 inch loaf pans or a 10 inch tube pan with greased parchment or heavy paper.

## Step 2

Sift together the flour, cinnamon, cloves, nutmeg, and salt.

**Step 3**

Cut the gumdrops in fourths. Fry the pecans in the 1 tablespoon butter or margarine. Mix pecans, raisins, and gumdrops together, and roll in 3/4 cup of flour mixture.

**Step 4**

In a large bowl, cream together 1 cup butter or margarine and white sugar. Mix in beaten eggs. Mix in the flour and spice mixture alternately with the applesauce. Dissolve soda in hot water, and stir into batter. Stir in the vanilla. Stir in nuts, gumdrops, and raisins.

**Step 5**

Bake for 2 hours. The baking time for the tube pan should be about 30 to 40 minutes longer. Test about 10 minutes before the longer time. You may not get a clean tester, but you will be able to tell if it is the candy gumdrop or dough. Cool. Wrap in foil.

**Nutrition Facts**

**Per Serving:**

328.7 calories; protein 3.2g 7% DV; carbohydrates 58.2g 19% DV; fat 10.4g 16% DV; cholesterol 31.8mg 11% DV; sodium 129.8mg 5% DV.

# Cranberry Pecan Cake

**Prep:** 20 mins **Cook:** 40 mins **Additional:** 30 mins **Total:** 1 hr 30 mins **Servings:** 12 **Yield:** 1 cake

**Ingredients**

- 3 cups frozen cranberries
- 1 cup pecans
- 1 cup white sugar
- 2 large eggs eggs
- 1 cup white sugar
- 1 cup all-purpose flour
- ½ cup butter, melted
- 2 tablespoons milk

**Directions**

**Step 1**

Preheat oven to 350 degrees F (175 degrees C). Generously grease a 2 quart rectangular baking dish.

**Step 2**

Spread the cranberries evenly over the bottom of the baking dish, and sprinkle the pecans over the cranberries. Spoon 1 cup of sugar over the cranberries and pecans.

**Step 3**

Place the eggs into the work bowl of an electric mixer, and beat on high speed about 1 minute, until the eggs are foamy. Beat in 1 cup of sugar, the flour, melted butter, and milk, and beat on Low until just mixed. The batter will be thick. Spread the batter evenly over the cranberry-pecan mixture.

**Step 4**

Bake in the preheated oven until the cake is lightly brown and a toothpick inserted near the center comes out clean, 40 to 45 minutes. Carefully invert the cake onto a serving plate, so the cranberry-pecan layer is on top. Let cool 30 minutes before serving.

**Nutrition Facts**

**Per Serving:**

327.4 calories; protein 3.3g 7% DV; carbohydrates 45.7g 15% DV; fat 15.8g 24% DV; cholesterol 51.5mg 17% DV; sodium 67.9mg 3% DV.

# Pecan Cheesecake

**Servings: 16 Yield:** 1 - 10 inch cheesecake

**Ingredients**

- 2 cups graham cracker crumbs
- ½ cup white sugar
- 1 teaspoon ground cinnamon
- ½ cup butter, melted
- 3 (8 ounce) packages cream cheese, softened
- 1 ¼ cups white sugar
- 3 large eggs eggs, room temperature
- ½ teaspoon vanilla extract
- ½ cup pecan liqueur

- 1 cup sour cream
- ¼ cup confectioners' sugar
- 1 teaspoon pecan liqueur
- 1 cup ground pecans
- ½ cup graham cracker crumbs
- 1 ½ tablespoons white sugar
- ½ teaspoon ground cinnamon
- ¾ cup pecan halves

**Directions**

**Step 1**

Combine 2 cups graham cracker crumbs, 1/2 cup white sugar, 1 teaspoon cinnamon, and melted butter or margarine. Press firmly into the bottom of a 10 inch springform pan.

**Step 2**

In a large bowl, blend the cream cheese and 1 1/4 cup white sugar with an electric mixer at medium speed until well blended. Add the eggs, one at a time, blending well. Add vanilla extract. Add 1/2 cup liqueur, and blend for 5 minutes. Pour the filling on top of the crust

## Step 3

Preheat the oven to 350 degrees F (175 degrees C). Bake for approximately 1 hour. The cake should be golden brown, and will have risen to the top of the pan. Turn off the heat, and let cool in the oven for 2 1/2 hours. When cool, remove the rim of the springform pan.

## Step 4

In a small bowl, mix the sour cream, confectioners' sugar, and 1 teaspoon liqueur together. Spoon onto the top of the cooled cheesecake.

## Step 5

In a small bowl, combine the finely ground pecans, finely ground graham cracker crumbs, 1 1/2 tablespoons white sugar, and cinnamon. Sprinkle the pecan topping on the cheesecake. Carefully press the pecan topping into the sides of the cheesecake. Garnish the top and sides with pecan halves.

**Nutrition Facts**

**Per Serving:**

493 calories; protein 6.7g 13% DV; carbohydrates 42.9g 14% DV; fat 33.1g 51% DV; cholesterol 102.7mg 34% DV; sodium 265.4mg 11% DV.

# Sweet Figgy Pudding

**Prep:** 15 mins **Cook:** 3 hrs **Total:** 3 hrs 15 mins **Servings:** 8 **Yield:** 8 servings

## Ingredients

- 1 cup all-purpose flour
- 1 cup soft bread crumbs
- 1 cup water
- 1 cup molasses
- 1 cup chopped dried figs
- 1 cup raisins
- ½ cup chopped walnuts
- ½ cup orange peel strips
- 1 teaspoon baking soda
- 1 teaspoon ground cinnamon
- 1 teaspoon ground cloves
- 1 teaspoon ground allspice
- 1 teaspoon ground nutmeg

## Directions

## Step 1

Grease the inside bowl of a double-boiler.

## Step 2

Mix flour, bread crumbs, water, molasses, figs, raisins, walnuts, orange peel, baking soda, cinnamon, cloves, allspice, and nutmeg together in a bowl until batter is well incorporated; spoon batter into the prepared double-boiler bowl and cover.

### Step 3

Fill the bottom half of a double boiler with water and bring to a boil; reduce heat and simmer. Place bowl in the simmering water and cover. Steam until pudding is cooked through, adding water as needed, 3 hours. Cool slightly with cover ajar before serving warm.

### Nutrition Facts

### Per Serving:

374 calories; protein 4.7g 9% DV; carbohydrates 81.3g 26% DV; fat 5.8g 9% DV; cholesterolmg; sodium 218.2mg 9% DV.

# Mini Red Velvet Cupcakes with Italian Meringue Frosting

**Prep:** 20 mins **Cook:** 15 mins **Total:** 35 mins **Servings:** 24 **Yield:** 2 dozen mini cupcakes

### Ingredients

- 1 ⅓ cups cake and pastry flour, sifted
- ⅔ cup granulated sugar
- 1 tablespoon unsweetened cocoa powder
- ½ teaspoon baking powder
- ¼ teaspoon baking soda
- ½ cup buttermilk

- ¼ cup butter, melted
- 1 egg
- 1 tablespoon red food colouring
- 1 teaspoon pure vanilla extract
- Edible gold flakes or sugar for garnish

### Italian Meringue Frosting:

- ⅓ cup granulated sugar
- ¼ cup water
- 2 large egg whites egg whites

- Pinch cream of tartar
- ½ teaspoon pure vanilla extract

### Directions

### Step 1

Preheat oven to 350 degrees F (175 degrees C). Grease 24 mini muffin cups or line with paper.

### Step 2

In a large bowl, whisk together cake and pastry flour, sugar, cocoa powder, baking powder and baking soda; set aside.

## Step 3

In another small bowl, whisk together buttermilk, melted butter, egg, food colouring and vanilla. Pour over flour mixture and whisk until smooth and well-combined. Divide batter among prepared muffin cups.

## Step 4

Bake in the preheated oven for about 15 minutes or until toothpick in centre comes out clean. Remove from pan and let cool completely on rack.

## Step 5

Italian Meringue Frosting: In a small saucepan, bring sugar and water to boil, stirring to dissolve sugar. Let mixture boil for 5 minutes.

## Step 6

Meanwhile, in a large bowl, beat egg whites with cream of tartar until soft peaks form. While beating, add the hot sugar syrup in a steady stream and beat for about 5 minutes or until glossy stiff peaks form. Beat in vanilla.

## Step 7

Frost the cupcakes and sprinkle with gold flakes or sugar as desired.

**Nutrition Facts**

**Per Serving:**

85.8 calories; protein 1.5g 3% DV; carbohydrates 15g 5% DV; fat 2.3g 4% DV; cholesterol 13mg 4% DV; sodium 50.1mg 2% DV.

# Santa's Favorite Cake

**Prep:** 45 mins **Cook:** 25 mins **Additional:** 1 hr **Total:** 2 hrs 10 mins **Servings:** 12 **Yield:** 1 - 3 layer cake

### Ingredients

- 1 (18.25 ounce) package white cake mix
- 3 large egg whites egg whites
- 1 ⅓ cups buttermilk
- 2 tablespoons vegetable oil
- 1 (9 ounce) package yellow cake mix
- ½ cup buttermilk
- 1 egg
- 1 ½ tablespoons unsweetened cocoa powder

- 2 tablespoons red food coloring
- 1 teaspoon cider vinegar
- 1 (8 ounce) package cream cheese, softened
- 1 cup margarine, softened
- 2 (16 ounce) packages confectioners' sugar
- 2 teaspoons peppermint extract

**Directions**

**Step 1**

Preheat oven to 350 degrees F (175 degrees C). Grease and flour three 9 inch round cake pans.

**Step 2**

In a large bowl, combine white cake mix, 3 egg whites, 1 1/3 cups buttermilk, and 2 tablespoons vegetable oil. Mix with an electric mixer for 2 minutes on high speed. In a separate bowl, combine yellow cake mix, 1/2 cup buttermilk, 1 egg, cocoa, red food coloring, and vinegar. Use an electric mixer to beat for 2 minutes on high speed.

**Step 3**

Spoon white batter alternately with red batter into the prepared cake pans. Swirl batter gently with a knife to create a marbled effect.

**Step 4**

Bake in preheated oven for 22 to 25 minutes, or until a wooden pick inserted into the centers comes out clean. Let cool in pans for at least 10 minutes before turning out onto a wire rack to cool completely.

**Step 5**

In a large bowl, beat cream cheese and margarine until smooth. Gradually blend in sugar until incorporated and smooth. Stir in peppermint extract. Spread peppermint cream cheese frosting between layers, and on top and sides of cake.

**Nutrition Facts**

**Per Serving:**

809.8 calories; protein 7.2g 14% DV; carbohydrates 126.9g 41% DV; fat 31.7g 49% DV; cholesterol 38mg 13% DV; sodium 711.2mg 28% DV.

# Snow on the Mountain

**Prep:** 20 mins **Cook:** 30 mins **Additional:** 1 hr 20 mins **Total:** 2 hrs 10 mins **Servings:** 8 **Yield:** 8 servings

**Ingredients**

- 1 cup dates, pitted and chopped
- 1 cup chopped walnuts
- ½ cup all-purpose flour
- 1 cup white sugar
- 4 large eggs eggs
- 1 teaspoon baking powder
- ¼ teaspoon salt
- 2 teaspoons vanilla extract
- 5 fruit, without seeds oranges, peeled and cut into 5 or 6 pieces
- 3 medium (7" to 7-7/8" long)s bananas, cut into 1 inch pieces
- ¼ cup white sugar
- 1 pint heavy whipping cream
- ¼ cup confectioners' sugar
- 1 teaspoon vanilla extract

**Directions**

**Step 1**

Preheat oven to 350 degrees F (175 degrees C). Grease and flour an 8 inch pan.

**Step 2**

In a medium bowl, beat together the eggs and 1 cup of sugar. Combine the flour, baking powder and salt, stir into the egg mixture. Then, stir in the dates, walnuts and vanilla. Pour into the prepared pan.

**Step 3**

Bake for 25 to 30 minutes in the preheated oven. Cool on the pan on a wire rack. When the cake is cooled, break into bite sized pieces. Stir the cake pieces together with the oranges, bananas and remaining sugar. Press into a medium sized bowl and chill for several hours.

**Step 4**

Invert cake onto a serving plate. Whip the heavy cream with the confectioners' sugar and vanilla until stiff. Spread over the entire cake.

**Nutrition Facts**

**Per Serving:**

659.4 calories; protein 9.6g 19% DV; carbohydrates 84.5g 27% DV; fat 34.6g 53% DV; cholesterol 174.5mg 58% DV; sodium 194.7mg 8% DV.

# Danish Rice Pudding with Almonds

**Prep:** 15 mins **Cook:** 25 mins **Additional:** 4 hrs **Total:** 4 hrs 40 mins **Servings:** 6 **Yield:** 6 servings

**Ingredients**

- 2 cups milk
- ⅓ cup Arborio rice
- ¼ cup chopped blanched almonds
- ¼ cup sherry

- ½ (.25 ounce) envelope unflavored gelatin
- ⅓ cup white sugar
- 1 teaspoon vanilla extract
- 1 cup heavy cream
- 1 (12 ounce) package frozen raspberries - thawed and drained

## Directions

### Step 1

In a saucepan, bring the milk to a boil, and then add rice. Reduce heat to simmer, and continue cooking for 20 minutes, stirring occasionally. Remove from heat, and set aside to cool to room temperature.

### Step 2

In a small saucepan, mix the sherry and gelatin; stir over low heat until the gelatin is dissolved. Stir in the sugar until completely dissolved, and then stir in vanilla. Stir into the rice with the chopped almonds. Refrigerate.

### Step 3

Pour cream into a bowl, and whip until light and fluffy soft peaks appear. Fold into chilled rice pudding. Serve in small bowls, topped with frozen raspberries.

## Nutrition Facts

### Per Serving:

364.4 calories; protein 6.5g 13% DV; carbohydrates 41.2g 13% DV; fat 19.4g 30% DV; cholesterol 60.9mg 20% DV; sodium 52.7mg 2% DV.

# Gingerbread Cheesecake

Prep: 30 mins Cook: 1 hr Additional: 5 hrs Total: 6 hrs 30 mins Servings: 16 Yield: 16 servings

## Ingredients

### Cheesecake:

- aluminum foil
- 2 cups gingerbread cookie crumbs
- ¼ cup unsalted butter, melted
- 3 (8 ounce) packages cream cheese, at room temperature
- 1 cup dark brown sugar
- ⅓ cup unsulphured molasses
- 1 tablespoon lemon juice
- 1 tablespoon vanilla extract
- 2 teaspoons ground ginger
- 1 ½ teaspoons ground cinnamon
- ½ teaspoon ground cloves
- ½ teaspoon ground nutmeg
- ¼ teaspoon ground allspice
- 1 pinch salt
- 3 large eggs eggs, room temperature

### Cinnamon Whipped Cream:

- 1 cup heavy whipping cream
- ¼ cup confectioners' sugar, or to taste
- ½ teaspoon vanilla extract
- ½ teaspoon cinnamon, or to taste
- 1 pinch salt

**Directions**

### Step 1

Preheat the oven to 350 degrees F (175 degrees C). Grease a 9-inch springform pan. Wrap the outside of the springform pan 3 to 4 times with aluminum foil.

### Step 2

Mix cookie crumbs and melted butter together until mixture resembles wet sand. Press into the prepared springform pan until bottom is evenly covered.

### Step 3

Combine cream cheese and brown sugar in a large bowl; beat with an electric mixer until smooth. Add molasses, lemon juice, vanilla extract, ginger, cinnamon, cloves, nutmeg, allspice, and salt; mix until well combined. Add eggs, 1 at a time, beating briefly after each addition until just combined. Pour batter over the crust in the pan. Tap the pan on the counter several times to remove any air bubbles.

### Step 4

Place the springform pan into a larger baking pan, and fill the baking pan with 1 inch hot water, making sure no water gets into the cheesecake batter.

### Step 5

Bake in the water bath in the preheated oven until the edges of the cheesecake are set and the middle jiggles slightly, about 1 hour. Turn off the oven without removing the cheesecake, leaving it inside until cooled, 1 to 2 hours.

### Step 6

Remove from the oven and water bath. Run the tip of a table knife around the edges of the springform pan before removing to a serving platter. Refrigerate until completely chilled, at least 4 hours.

### Step 7

Combine whipping cream, powdered sugar, vanilla extract, cinnamon, and salt for the cinnamon whipped cream in a large bowl. Beat with an electric mixer on medium-high speed until stiff peaks form; do not overmix.

### Step 8

Top cheesecake with whipped cream just before serving.

**Nutrition Facts**

**Per Serving:**

359 calories; protein 5.2g 10% DV; carbohydrates 28g 9% DV; fat 25.8g 40% DV; cholesterol 112.4mg 38% DV; sodium 204mg 8% DV.

# Simple Christmas Rum Cake

**Prep:** 15 mins **Cook:** 40 mins **Additional:** 1 hr 10 mins **Total:** 2 hrs 5 mins **Servings:** 16 **Yield:** 1 cake

## Ingredients

- cooking spray
- 1 (18.25 ounce) package yellow cake mix with pudding (such as Betty Crocker)
- 3 large eggs eggs
- ⅓ cup rum
- ½ cup water
- ½ cup vegetable oil
- ¼ cup rum
- ¼ cup water
- 1 cup white sugar
- ½ cup butter
- 1 teaspoon confectioners' sugar for sprinkling

## Directions

### Step 1

Preheat oven to 350 degrees F (175 degrees C). Spray a fluted tube pan (such as a Bundt) with cooking spray.

### Step 2

Place the cake mix, eggs, 1/3 cup of rum, 1/2 cup of water, and the vegetable oil into a large bowl. Beat until smooth with an electric mixer on low speed, about 3 minutes.

### Step 3

Pour the batter into the prepared pan.

### Step 4

Bake in the preheated oven until the cake has risen and the top is lightly golden brown, about 40 minutes. A toothpick inserted into the center of the cake should come out clean.

### Step 5

While cake is baking, make the glaze. In a saucepan over medium heat, combine 1/4 cup of rum, 1/4 cup of water, sugar, and butter. Stir and heat until all the sugar has dissolved and the butter is melted. Turn off heat.

## Step 6

Remove the cake from the oven. While still hot and in the pan, poke the cake all over with a long skewer to make many deep holes.

## Step 7

Pour the glaze over the hot cake. Allow the cake to cool until the cake separates slightly from the side of the pan, 10 to 12 minutes.

## Step 8

Line a jellyroll pan or large baking sheet with waxed paper. Carefully place the lined pan over the top of the cake pan, and flip the cake pan over to release the cake onto the waxed paper. If desired, transfer cake to a serving platter.

## Step 9

Let the cake cool thoroughly and sprinkle lightly with confectioners' sugar before slicing.

**Nutrition Facts**

**Per Serving:**

331.9 calories; protein 2.7g 5% DV; carbohydrates 38g 12% DV; fat 17.3g 27% DV; cholesterol 50.8mg 17% DV; sodium 266.7mg 11% DV.

# Chocolate-Raspberry Cheesecake

**Prep:** 30 mins **Cook:** 1 hr **Additional:** 4 hrs 30 mins **Total:** 6 hrs **Servings:** 16 **Yield:** 16 servings, 1 piece (84 g) each

## Ingredients

- 1 (150 g) package round shortbread cookies, finely crushed
- 1 tablespoon butter, melted
- 3 (250 g) packages PHILADELPHIA Chocolate Brick Cream Cheese, softened
- ¾ cup white sugar, divided
- 3 large eggs eggs
- 4 cups raspberries
- 1 tablespoon cornstarch
- 1 tablespoon water

## Directions

### Step 1

Heat oven to 350 degrees F (175 degrees C).

### Step 2

Mix cookie crumbs and butter; press onto bottom of 9-inch springform pan.

### Step 3

Beat cream cheese and 1/2 cup sugar in large bowl with mixer until blended. Add eggs, 1 at a time, mixing on low speed after each just until blended; pour over crust.

### Step 4

Bake 40 to 45 minutes or until centre is almost set. Run knife around rim of pan to loosen cake; cool before removing rim. Refrigerate cheesecake 4 hours.

### Step 5

Meanwhile, cook raspberries and remaining sugar in saucepan on medium-high heat 12 to 14 minutes or until slightly thickened, stirring frequently. Mix cornstarch and water until blended. Add to raspberry mixture; cook and stir 1 minutes or until thickened. Pour through fine-mesh strainer into bowl; refrigerate until ready to serve.

### Step 6

Serve cheesecake topped with raspberry sauce.

**Nutrition Facts**

**Per Serving:**

295.9 calories; protein 5g 10% DV; carbohydrates 31.2g 10% DV; fat 17.3g 27% DV; cholesterol 82.6mg 28% DV; sodium 207.5mg 8% DV.

# Blue Ribbon Whipping Cream Pound Cake

**Servings:** 16 **Yield:** 1 - 10 inch tube pan

### Ingredients

- 2 ½ cups white sugar
- 1 cup butter
- 7 large eggs eggs
- 6 tablespoons cornstarch
- 2 ⅝ cups all-purpose flour
- 1 cup heavy whipping cream
- 2 tablespoons vanilla extract

**Directions**

### Step 1

Preheat oven to 350 degrees F(175 degrees C). Grease and flour a 10 inch tube pan. Set aside.

### Step 2

Cream together the sugar and butter until light. Continue beating and add 7 eggs, one at a time; beating well after each egg

**Step 3**

In a separate bowl, mix together flour and cornstarch. Beat half of the flour mixture into the egg and sugar mixture.

**Step 4**

Beat in 1/2 cup whipping cream, and then beat in the remainder of the flour mixture. Finish by beating in 1/2 cup more of whipping cream and vanilla.

**Step 5**

Pour into prepared pan and bake for about 60 to 75 minutes. Cool on rack for 10 minutes before turning it out onto a serving plate.

**Nutrition Facts**

**Per Serving:**

396 calories; protein 5.3g 11% DV; carbohydrates 50.4g 16% DV; fat 19.4g 30% DV; cholesterol 132.3mg 44% DV; sodium 118.8mg 5% DV.

# Delicious Whole Wheat Fruitcake Cookies

**Prep:** 20 mins **Cook:** 15 mins **Total:** 35 mins **Servings:** 18 **Yield:** 1 9x5 inch loaf or 3 dozen cookies

**Ingredients**

- 1 cup packed brown sugar
- 1 cup water
- 1 cup raisins
- 2 tablespoons butter
- ½ teaspoon salt
- 1 ½ cups whole wheat flour
- ¾ teaspoon baking soda
- ½ teaspoon ground ginger
- 1 teaspoon ground cinnamon
- ½ cup dates, pitted and chopped
- ½ cup candied mixed fruit peel, chopped
- ½ cup chopped nuts
- ½ cup chopped dried mixed fruit

**Directions**

**Step 1**

Preheat oven to 350 degrees F (175 degrees C). Grease one 5x9 inch loaf pan.

**Step 2**

In a saucepan over medium heat, cook together the sugar, water, raisins, butter and salt. Remove from heat and allow to cool.

**Step 3**

Sift together the flour, soda, ginger and cinnamon. Stir into the cooled cooked mixture.

**Step 4**

Add the chopped dates, mixed peels, nuts and dried fruit.

**Step 5**

Pour into loaf pan and bake for 1 hour or drop by the teaspoon on a cookie sheet and bake for 15 minutes.

**Nutrition Facts**

**Per Serving:**

183.6 calories; protein 2.5g 5% DV; carbohydrates 37.8g 12% DV; fat 3.8g 6% DV; cholesterol 3.4mg 1% DV; sodium 132.6mg 5% DV.

# Easy Eggnog Pound Cake

**Prep:** 10 mins **Cook:** 40 mins **Additional:** 10 mins **Total:** 1 hr **Servings:** 12 **Yield:** 1 pound cake

**Ingredients**

- 1 (18.25 ounce) package yellow cake mix
- ¾ cup butter, softened
- ¾ cup eggnog
- 1 (3.5 ounce) package instant vanilla pudding mix
- 4 large eggs eggs
- ½ teaspoon ground nutmeg
- 1 tablespoon confectioners' sugar, or as needed

**Directions**

**Step 1**

Preheat oven to 350 degrees F (175 degrees C). Grease and flour a 10-inch fluted cake pan.

**Step 2**

Beat cake mix, butter, eggnog, and pudding mix together in a bowl with an electric mixer until just moistened. Add eggs and nutmeg; beat until batter is smooth, about 4 minutes. Pour batter into prepared cake pan.

**Step 3**

Bake in the preheated oven until a toothpick inserted in the center of the cake comes out clean, 40 to 45 minutes. Cool in the pan for 10 minutes before removing to a wire rack to cool completely. Dust with confectioners' sugar.

## Nutrition Facts

### Per Serving:

366.2 calories; protein 4.7g 10% DV; carbohydrates 44.2g 14% DV; fat 19.4g 30% DV; cholesterol 102.7mg 34% DV; sodium 514.4mg 21% DV.

# Eggnog Pound Cake

**Prep:** 35 mins **Cook:** 1 hr 5 mins **Total:** 1 hr 40 mins **Servings:** 16 **Yield:** 1 - 10 inch tube or Bundt pan

## Ingredients

- ¼ cup dried blueberries
- ¼ cup chopped dried cherries
- ¼ cup dried cranberries
- 2 tablespoons brandy
- 3 cups all-purpose flour
- 2 teaspoons baking powder
- ¼ teaspoon salt
- ⅛ teaspoon freshly grated nutmeg

- 1 cup unsalted butter, softened
- 2 cups white sugar
- 3 large eggs eggs
- 1 teaspoon vanilla extract
- 1 cup eggnog
- 2 tablespoons brandy
- 2 tablespoons water
- ¾ cup white sugar

## Directions

### Step 1

In a small bowl, combine dried blueberries, dried cherries, dried cranberries, and 2 tablespoons brandy. Soak for 15 minutes.

### Step 2

Preheat oven to 325 degrees F (165 degrees C). Grease and flour a 10 inch tube pan or Bundt pan. Sift together the flour, baking powder, salt, and nutmeg; set aside.

### Step 3

In a large bowl, cream together the butter and 2 cups sugar until light and fluffy. Beat in the eggs one at a time, then stir in the vanilla. Beat in the flour mixture alternately with the eggnog, mixing just until incorporated. Fold in soaked fruit mixture. Spread batter into prepared pan.

### Step 4

Bake in the preheated oven for 55 minutes, or until a toothpick inserted into the center of the cake comes out clean. Let cool in pan for 10 minutes, then turn out onto a wire rack.

### Step 5

In a small bowl, mix together brandy, water, and 3/4 cup sugar. With pastry brush, brush entire surface of cake with glaze. Cool completely before serving.

### Nutrition Facts

### Per Serving:

386.8 calories; protein 4.5g 9% DV; carbohydrates 59.5g 19% DV; fat 13.9g 21% DV; cholesterol 74.7mg 25% DV; sodium 106.2mg 4% DV.

# Pumpkin Spice Ring

**Servings:** 10 **Yield:** 10 servings

### Ingredients

- 1 (18.25 ounce) package angel food cake mix
- 1 cup pumpkin puree
- ½ teaspoon pumpkin pie spice

### Directions

### Step 1

Combine pumpkin and pumpkin pie spice, and mix well. Set aside.

### Step 2

Mix cake as directed on package. Fold in pumpkin mixture. Pour into an ungreased tube pan.

### Step 3

Bake at 350 degrees F (175 degrees C) until lightly browned, using the box directions as a guide to cooking time.

### Nutrition Facts

### Per Serving:

196.9 calories; protein 4.3g 9% DV; carbohydrates 43.7g 14% DV; fat 0.1g; cholesterolmg; sodium 502.9mg 20% DV.

# Hot Milk Sponge Cake

**Prep:** 15 mins **Cook:** 50 mins **Total:** 1 hr 5 mins **Servings:** 12 **Yield:** 1 large loaf cake

## Ingredients

- ¾ cup milk
- 2 tablespoons butter
- 3 large eggs eggs
- 1 ½ cups white sugar
- 1 ½ cups all-purpose flour
- 1 ½ teaspoons baking powder
- 1 teaspoon vanilla extract

## Directions

### Step 1

Preheat oven to 350 degrees F (175 degrees C). Grease one large loaf pan or one 10 inch tube pan.

### Step 2

In a saucepan over medium-low heat, combine the milk and the butter. Do not boil.

### Step 3

In a large bowl beat the eggs until light colored. Gradually add the sugar to the eggs then stir in the flour and baking powder. Stir in the hot milk and butter. Beat only until combined. Stir in the vanilla. Pour the batter into the prepared pan.

### Step 4

Bake at 350 degrees F (175 degrees C) for 45 to 50 minutes. Let cake cool in pan for 10 minutes. Remove cake from the pan and cool on a wire rack.

## Nutrition Facts

### Per Serving:

197.4 calories; protein 3.7g 7% DV; carbohydrates 37.9g 12% DV; fat 3.6g 6% DV; cholesterol 52.8mg 18% DV; sodium 98.7mg 4% DV.

# Poor Man's Cake

**Prep:** 10 mins **Cook:** 1 hr 40 mins **Total:** 1 hr 50 mins **Servings:** 18 **Yield:** 1 9x13-inch cake

## Ingredients

- 1 cup cold water
- 1 cup packed brown sugar
- 2 cups raisins
- ½ cup lard

- ½ teaspoon salt
- ½ teaspoon ground cinnamon
- ½ teaspoon ground nutmeg
- ¼ teaspoon ground cloves

- 1 ¾ cups all-purpose flour
- 1 teaspoon baking soda
- 1 teaspoon vanilla extract

**Directions**

**Step 1**

Preheat oven to 350 degrees F (175 degrees C). Lightly grease one 9 x 13 inch pan.

**Step 2**

Place cold water, brown sugar, raisins, lard, salt, cinnamon, nutmeg, and cloves in a large saucepan. Bring this combination to a boil. Let simmer for a full 6 minutes, then allow mixture to cool to lukewarm. Set aside.

**Step 3**

In small mixing bowl, combine flour and soda. Gradually add the dry ingredients to the cooled mixture. Add vanilla, and blend into batter. Pour batter into prepared pan.

**Step 4**

Bake in the preheated oven for 90 to 120 minutes, or until a toothpick inserted into the center of the cake comes out clean. Allow to cool. Store for at least a week before cutting. This cake will remain moist for months.

**Nutrition Facts**

**Per Serving:**

191.6 calories; protein 1.8g 4% DV; carbohydrates 34.2g 11% DV; fat 5.9g 9% DV; cholesterol 5.4mg 2% DV; sodium 140.1mg 6% DV.

# Gingerbread Pound Cake

**Prep:** 15 mins **Cook:** 1 hr **Additional:** 40 mins **Total:** 1 hr 55 mins **Servings:** 12 **Yield:** 1 Bundt(R) cake

**Ingredients**

- 1 cup unsalted butter, softened
- 1 cup white sugar
- 5 large eggs
- 2 cups all-purpose flour
- 1 teaspoon ground ginger

- 1 teaspoon ground cinnamon
- 1 teaspoon ground cloves
- ½ teaspoon baking soda
- 1 cup molasses
- ½ cup sour cream

- Lemon Sauce (Optional):
- 1 cup water
- ½ cup white sugar
- 2 tablespoons cornstarch

- ⅓ cup lemon juice
- 1 tablespoon unsalted butter
- 2 teaspoons grated lemon zest
- ⅛ cup sifted powdered sugar, or to taste

## Directions

### Step 1

Preheat the oven to 325 degrees F (165 degrees C). Grease and flour a 12-cup fluted tube pan (such as Bundt) well.

### Step 2

Beat butter in a mixing bowl on medium speed until soft and creamy, about 2 minutes; gradually add 1 cup white sugar, beating at medium speed for 5 to 7 minutes. Add eggs one at a time, beating just until yellow disappears; batter may look a bit curdled.

### Step 3

Combine flour, ginger, cinnamon, cloves, and baking soda in a separate bowl. Combine molasses and sour cream in another bowl. Add dry ingredients to the batter alternately with molasses mixture, beginning and ending with dry ingredients. Mix on low speed until each addition is just blended. Pour into the prepared pan.

### Step 4

Bake in the preheated oven until a toothpick inserted into the center of the cake comes out clean, about 1 hour. Cool cake in the pan on a wire rack for 10 to 15 minutes; remove cake from pan and cool completely, about 30 minutes more.

### Step 5

While cake cools, combine water, white sugar, and cornstarch in a saucepan; cook over medium heat, stirring constantly, until smooth and thickened. Stir in lemon juice, butter, and lemon zest and cook until warmed through.

### Step 6

Sprinkle cooled cake with powdered sugar and serve with lemon sauce.

## Nutrition Facts

### Per Serving:

459.8 calories; protein 5.3g 11% DV; carbohydrates 65.4g 21% DV; fat 20.7g 32% DV; cholesterol 124.9mg 42% DV; sodium 100.7mg 4% DV.

# Chocolate-Peppermint Cheesecake

**Prep:** 20 mins **Cook:** 45 mins **Additional:** 5 hrs **Total:** 6 hrs 5 mins **Servings:** 16 **Yield:** 16 servings, 1 slice (82g) each

## Ingredients

- 1 ¼ cups chocolate cookie baking crumbs
- ¼ cup butter, melted
- 3 (250 g) packages PHILADELPHIA Chocolate Brick Cream Cheese, softened
- ¾ cup white sugar
- 1 teaspoon peppermint extract
- 3 large eggs eggs
- ½ cup whipping cream
- 1 tablespoon white sugar
- 1 candy cane, crushed

## Directions

### Step 1

Heat oven to 350 degrees F (175 degrees C).

### Step 2

Mix baking crumbs and butter; press onto bottom of 9-inch springform pan.

### Step 3

Beat cream cheese and 3/4 cup sugar in large bowl with mixer until blended. Add extract; mix well. Add eggs, 1 at a time, mixing on low speed after each just until blended; pour over crust.

### Step 4

Bake 40 to 45 minutes or until centre is almost set. Run knife around rim of pan to loosen cake; cool before removing rim. Refrigerate cheesecake 4 hours.

### Step 5

Beat cream in separate bowl with mixer on high speed until soft peaks form. Gradually add remaining sugar, beating until stiff peaks form; spoon over cheesecake. Sprinkle with crushed candy.

### Nutrition Facts

### Per Serving:

325 calories; protein 4.9g 10% DV; carbohydrates 30.2g 10% DV; fat 21g 32% DV; cholesterol 96.8mg 32% DV; sodium 234.3mg 9% DV.

# Chesscakes

**Prep:** 20 mins **Cook:** 30 mins **Additional:** 10 mins **Total:** 1 hr **Servings:** 24 **Yield:** 24 cupcakes

## Ingredients

- 1 (18.25 ounce) package white cake mix
- 2 (9 inch) unbaked pie crusts
- 1 (10 ounce) jar raspberry preserves

## Directions

### Step 1

Preheat oven to 350 degrees F (175 degrees C). You will need two un-greased, 12-cup muffin tins for this recipe. (You may want to spray tops of muffin pans with nonstick cooking spray so cake does not stick).

### Step 2

Prepare cake mix according to package directions; set aside. Roll out pastry dough to 18 inch thickness. Using a floured, round cookie cutter that is slightly bigger than the muffin cups, cut 24 circles of dough. Place one dough circle in each muffin cup, pressing dough gently into bottom and sides. Dough should come about halfway up the sides of each muffin cup.

### Step 3

Place a rounded tablespoon of raspberry jam into each pastry-lined cup. Pour prepared cake batter into each cup over jam and pastry, filling just to the top of each cup.

### Step 4

Bake in preheated oven for 25 to 30 minutes or until a toothpick inserted into the cake comes out clean. Let cool briefly in pans, then loosen with knife and remove cakes to wire rack to cool completely.

## Nutrition Facts

### Per Serving:

195.7 calories; protein 1.9g 4% DV; carbohydrates 31g 10% DV; fat 7.3g 11% DV; cholesterolmg; sodium 219.3mg 9% DV.

# Christmas Cranberry Cake with Amaretto

**Prep:** 20 mins **Cook:** 55 mins **Total:** 1 hr 15 mins **Servings:** 12 **Yield:** 1 10-inch fluted tube cake

## Ingredients

- 1 (15.25 ounce) package yellow cake mix
- 1 (3.4 ounce) package instant vanilla pudding mix
- 5 large eggs eggs
- ½ cup amaretto liqueur

- ½ cup vegetable oil
- ½ cup milk
- 2 cups chopped cranberries
- 1 cup flaked coconut
- 1 cup walnuts, chopped

### Glaze:

- ¾ cup white sugar
- ½ cup amaretto liqueur

- 1 tablespoon butter

## Directions

### Step 1

Preheat the oven to 350 degrees F (175 degrees C). Grease and flour a fluted tube pan (such as Bundt).

### Step 2

Mix yellow cake mix, pudding mix, eggs, amaretto, oil, and milk together in a bowl. Beat using an electric mixer on medium speed for 2 to 3 minutes. Fold in cranberries, coconut, and walnuts. Pour into the prepared pan.

### Step 3

Bake in the preheated oven until a toothpick inserted into the center comes out clean, about 55 minutes.

### Step 4

Meanwhile, combine sugar, amaretto, and butter for glaze in a small saucepan. Bring to a boil; continue to boil until sugar is dissolved, 2 to 3 minutes.

### Step 5

Remove cake from the oven and glaze immediately.

### Nutrition Facts

### Per Serving:

537.9 calories; protein 6.3g 13% DV; carbohydrates 65.3g 21% DV; fat 24.9g 38% DV; cholesterol 81.6mg 27% DV; sodium 410.6mg 16% DV.

# Angel Food Roll with Cranberry Filling

**Prep:** 20 mins **Cook:** 7 mins **Total:** 27 mins **Servings:** 10 **Yield:** 10 servings

## Ingredients

- 1 ⅛ cups castor sugar or superfine sugar, divided
- ¾ cup sifted cake flour
- ¼ teaspoon salt
- 9 large egg whites egg whites
- 1 ½ teaspoons vanilla extract
- ¾ teaspoon cream of tartar
- ¼ cup confectioners' sugar for dusting
- 1 cup white sugar
- 2 ⅓ cups fresh or frozen cranberries
- 6 tablespoons water
- 2 tablespoons cornstarch
- ½ cup heavy cream
- 3 tablespoons confectioners' sugar

## Directions

### Step 1

Preheat the oven to 300 degrees F (150 degrees C). Lightly grease a 10x15 inch jellyroll pan with cooking spray. Line with parchment paper.

### Step 2

In a medium bowl, whisk together 1/2 cup of superfine sugar, cake flour and salt. Set aside. In a separate bowl, whip egg whites until foamy. Add vanilla and cream of tartar, and continue to whip. Gradually sprinkle in the remaining superfine sugar while continuing to whip the egg whites to firm peaks. Sift the flour mixture over the egg whites and fold in by hand using a rubber spatula. Spread the batter evenly in the prepared pan.

### Step 3

Bake for 20 minutes in the preheated oven, or until the center of the cake springs back when lightly pressed. Cool in the pan over a wire rack. Generously sift sugar over the top of the cake, and cover with a clean towel. Run a spatula around the outside of the cake in the pan to loosen, and turn out onto the towel. Remove the parchment paper from the back of the cake, then place it back on loosely. Roll up with the towel loosely from short end to short end, and allow to cool in the rolled position.

### Step 4

In a saucepan over medium heat, combine 1 cup of white sugar, cranberries and water. Simmer until the cranberries burst, about 5 minutes. Whisk in the cornstarch, and simmer just until thick, about 2 minutes. Transfer to a bowl, cover and refrigerate.

### Step 5

Unroll the cake so that it is sitting flat on the towel. Spread the cooled cranberry filling over the top, leaving 1/2 inch border. Use the towel to help you keep a grip on the cake for an even roll. Roll up from short end to short end and place seam side down onto a platter. Refrigerate until serving.

**Step 6**

Whip cream with confectioners' sugar until soft peaks form. Serve slices of cake with a dollop of sweetened whipped cream.

**Nutrition Facts**

**Per Serving:**

298.4 calories; protein 4.5g 9% DV; carbohydrates 61.1g 20% DV; fat 4.5g 7% DV; cholesterol 16.3mg 5% DV; sodium 114.1mg 5% DV.

# Noel Fruitcake

**Prep:** 30 mins **Cook:** 3 hrs 30 mins **Additional:** 2 weeks 5 days **Total:** 2 weeks 5 days **Servings:** 16 **Yield:** 1 10-inch cake

**Ingredients**

- 3 ½ cups sifted all-purpose flour
- 1 ¼ teaspoons baking powder
- 1 teaspoon salt
- 2 teaspoons ground cinnamon
- ¼ teaspoon ground cloves
- 1 ¼ cups raisins
- 1 cup chopped pecans
- 12 ounces dried apricots, chopped
- 8 ounces candied cherries, halved

- 4 ounces candied lemon peel
- 4 ounces candied orange peel
- ½ cup orange juice
- 1 cup jellied cranberry sauce
- 1 ½ cups shortening
- 2 ½ cups packed light brown sugar
- 5 large eggs eggs
- 1 ½ cups chopped cranberries

**Directions**

**Step 1**

Preheat oven to 300 degrees F (150 degrees C). Grease and flour a 10-inch tube pan. Line with parchment paper and grease the paper.

**Step 2**

In a medium bowl, sift flour, baking powder, salt, cinnamon and cloves together. Add raisins, pecans, apricots, cherries, lemon and orange peels. Toss to mix.

**Step 3**

In a small bowl, beat the orange juice and jellied cranberry sauce together until smooth. Set aside.

**Step 4**

In a large bowl, beat shortening, brown sugar and eggs together until fluffy. Add flour mixture alternately with the orange juice mixture, beginning and ending with the flour. Stir in the chopped cranberries just until the ingredients are well blended.

**Step 5**

Turn batter into the prepared pan. Bake for 3 1/2 to 4 hours or until the cake is golden brown. Cool cake in the pan. Remove from the pan and remove the paper. Store the cooled cake several weeks in a covered container to mellow flavors. You may also wrap the cake in a brandy-, whisky-, or rum-soaked cheesecloth before storing. If desired, garnish with orange slices and cranberries.

**Nutrition Facts**

**Per Serving:**

665.4 calories; protein 6.7g 13% DV; carbohydrates 106.8g 34% DV; fat 26.2g 40% DV; cholesterol 58.1mg 19% DV; sodium 238.8mg 10% DV.

# No-Bake Chocolate Yule Log with Chocolate Mushrooms

**Servings:** 10 **Yield:** 10 servings

### Ingredients

- 1 pint heavy cream
- 3 tablespoons unsweetened cocoa powder
- 5 tablespoons orange-flavored liqueur, such as Grand Marnier or Cointreau, divided
- 1 tablespoon sugar
- ¾ cup low-sugar orange marmalade
- 1 (9 ounce) box Nabisco Famous Chocolate Wafers
- 8 eaches nonpareils (or use chocolate stars or small Peppermint Patties)
- 8 eaches dark chocolate kisses, foil removed
- 1 (6 ounce) container raspberries

### Directions

**Step 1**

Beat cream, cocoa, 3 Tbs. liqueur and sugar to stiff peaks in a large bowl. Set aside. Mix marmalade with 2 Tbs. liqueur in a medium bowl. Select a platter long and wide enough to fit a 12-inch yule log with two 'knots.'

**Step 2**

On flat side of the first wafer, spread a scant teaspoon of marmalade and 1 1/2 tsps. of the cream mixture over entire surface, then top with another wafer, flat side up. Repeat until you have about 3 inches of wafers. Stand stack on its side at a slight angle on the serving platter. Keep adding to log until 16 wafers remain.

### Step 3

Stack 8 wafers, also on a slight angle, on each side of the log to form two knots.

### Step 4

Spread remaining whipped cream mix over whole log, coating completely, then create 'bark' by running fork tines along the log and each knot. Cover gently with plastic wrap and refrigerate at least 3 hours or overnight.

### Step 5

Using a toothpick or ice pick, make a small hole in the bottom of each nonpareil. Stick a chocolate kiss into each hole to form mushrooms. Decorate log with clusters of mushrooms, and scatter raspberries around the platter. Slice and serve.

### Nutrition Facts

### Per Serving:

388.8 calories; protein 3.5g 7% DV; carbohydrates 42g 14% DV; fat 22.9g 35% DV; cholesterol 66.2mg 22% DV; sodium 171mg 7% DV.

# Cranberry Cake Rolls

**Prep:** 30 mins **Additional:** 1 hr **Total:** 1 hr 30 mins **Servings:** 20 **Yield:** 20 servings (1 slice each)

### Ingredients

- PAM Baking Spray
- ½ cup confectioners' sugar, sifted
- 1 (15.25 ounce) package yellow cake mix
- 4 large eggs eggs
- ½ cup water
- 4 cups fresh or thawed frozen cranberries
- 1 ⅓ cups granulated sugar
- 1 ½ cups chopped pecans
- ½ cup orange marmalade, melted
- Reddi-wip Extra Creamy Whipped Cream

### Directions

### Step 1

Preheat oven to 350 degrees F. Spray 2 (15x10x1-inch) baking pans with baking spray. Line with parchment paper; spray with additional baking spray. Set aside. Sprinkle 2 clean kitchen towels with 1/4 cup each confectioners' sugar; set aside.

## Step 2

Beat cake mix, eggs and water in large bowl with electric mixer on low speed 30 seconds or until well blended. Beat on medium speed 2 minutes. Pour evenly into prepared pans.

## Step 3

Bake 12 to 15 minutes or until wooden pick inserted in centers comes out clean. Run knife or small spatula around rims of pans to loosen cakes. Immediately invert each cake onto a prepared towel; remove pan. Carefully peel off paper. Starting at one of the short sides, roll up each cake and towel to form 2 separate rolls. Cool completely on wire racks.

## Step 4

Meanwhile, combine cranberries and granulated sugar in medium saucepan; cook over medium heat 10 minutes or until juice of cranberries is released and sugar is dissolved, stirring occasionally. Stir in pecans. Cool completely.

## Step 5

Unroll cakes. Spread 1/2 cup marmalade evenly over each cake to within 1 inch of edges; top evenly with cranberry mixture. Re-roll cakes, using towels as guide. Trim ends of each cake. Cut each cake into 10 slices. Top each slice with a serving of Reddi-wip. Serve immediately.

**Nutrition Facts**

**Per Serving:**

286.8 calories; protein 3.1g 6% DV; carbohydrates 44.2g 14% DV; fat 12.5g 19% DV; cholesterol 47.8mg 16% DV; sodium 161mg 6% DV.

# Dark Gingerbread with Maple Whipped Cream

**Prep:** 20 mins **Cook:** 30 mins **Additional:** 10 mins **Total:** 1 hr **Servings:** 8 **Yield:** 1 9-inch cake

**Ingredients**

**Cake:**

- 1 ½ cups all-purpose flour
- 1 teaspoon ground cinnamon
- ¾ teaspoon ground ginger
- ½ teaspoon baking soda

137

- ½ teaspoon baking powder
- ½ teaspoon salt
- ½ cup unsalted butter, softened
- ⅓ cup dark brown sugar, packed
- ⅓ cup dark corn syrup
- ⅓ cup molasses
- 1 egg
- ½ cup hot water
- ¼ cup chopped crystallized ginger
- Whipped Cream Topping:
- 1 cup heavy whipping cream, chilled
- 2 tablespoons pure maple syrup

**Directions**

**Step 1**

Preheat oven to 350 degrees F (175 degrees C). Grease a 9-inch round or square pan and line bottom with parchment paper.

**Step 2**

Whisk flour, cinnamon, ground ginger, baking soda, baking powder, and salt together in a large bowl.

**Step 3**

Beat butter and brown sugar together in another large bowl with an electric mixer until light and fluffy, 3 to 4 minutes. Add corn syrup, molasses, and egg; beat until smooth. Pour in hot water slowly while continuing to beat. Add flour mixture gradually, mixing until batter is well-blended and smooth. Stir in crystallized ginger. Pour batter into the pan.

**Step 4**

Bake in the preheated oven until a toothpick inserted into the center comes out clean, 30 to 35 minutes. Cool in the pan, about 10 minutes. Run a knife around the edges and carefully invert onto a wire rack. Cut into wedges or squares.

**Step 5**

Whip heavy cream and maple syrup together in a large bowl until stiff peaks form. Serve whipped cream topping with cake.

**Nutrition Facts**

**Per Serving:**

436.2 calories; protein 4g 8% DV; carbohydrates 54.8g 18% DV; fat 23.4g 36% DV; cholesterol 94.5mg 32% DV; sodium 308mg 12% DV.

# Gingerbread Cheesecake Bars

**Prep:** 25 mins **Cook:** 25 mins **Additional:** 4 hrs **Total:** 4 hrs 50 mins **Servings:** 24 **Yield:** 24 bars

## Ingredients

### Cookie Base:

- 2 ¼ cups all-purpose flour
- 2 teaspoons ground ginger
- 1 teaspoon baking soda
- 1 teaspoon ground cinnamon
- ½ teaspoon ground cloves
- ¼ teaspoon salt

- ¾ cup margarine, softened
- 1 cup white sugar
- 1 egg
- ¼ cup molasses
- 1 tablespoon water

### Filling:

- 2 (8 ounce) packages cream cheese
- ½ cup powdered sugar
- ½ cup brown sugar
- 6 tablespoons molasses
- 2 teaspoons ground ginger

- 2 teaspoons ground cinnamon
- ½ teaspoon ground nutmeg
- ½ teaspoon ground cloves
- 3 cups whipped topping
- 2 tablespoons whipped topping, or to taste

## Directions

### Step 1

Preheat the oven to 350 degrees F (175 degrees C).

### Step 2

Sift together flour, ginger, baking soda, cinnamon, cloves, and salt for the cookie base in a bowl.

### Step 3

Cream margarine and white sugar in a large bowl with an electric mixer until light and fluffy. Add egg and beat until well combined. Stir in molasses and water. Gradually stir flour mixture into the molasses mixture. Transfer dough to a 9x13-inch pan, patting it down so it covers the entire bottom of the pan.

### Step 4

Bake in the preheated oven until lightly browned, 25 to 30 minutes. Allow to cool completely.

### Step 5

Beat cream cheese, powdered sugar, and brown sugar for the filling in a large bowl with an electric mixer until smooth. Add molasses, ginger, cinnamon, nutmeg, and cloves and stir, scraping down the sides of the bowl, until mixture is smooth. Fold in 3 cups whipped topping until well combined. Spread filling into the cooled cookie base. Cover with plastic wrap and refrigerate until set, at least 4 hours or overnight.

**Step 6**

Garnish with remaining whipped topping before serving.

**Nutrition Facts**

**Per Serving:**

261.5 calories; protein 3.2g 7% DV; carbohydrates 31.2g 10% DV; fat 14.2g 22% DV; cholesterol 34.2mg 11% DV; sodium 215.2mg 9% DV.

# Saffron and Cointreau Cheesecake on Gingerbread

**Prep:** 40 mins **Cook:** 5 mins **Additional:** 8 hrs 20 mins **Total:** 9 hrs 5 mins **Servings:** 12 **Yield:** 1 cheesecake

**Ingredients**

- 1 (8 ounce) package ginger nut cookies (biscuits)
- ½ cup butter, melted
- ¼ cup Cointreau or other orange liqueur
- ½ (.5 gram) packet saffron threads

- 5 (3 ounce) packages cream cheese
- ½ cup honey
- 1 ½ tablespoons finely-grated orange zest
- 1 ¾ cups heavy cream

**Directions**

**Step 1**

Place the cookies and butter in a blender. Blend until you have a slightly-moist and crumbly mixture. Press the crumbs into the base of a 9 inch springform pan; refrigerate.

**Step 2**

Heat the Cointreau in a small saucepan until it begins to steam; add the saffron threads. Remove from heat and allow to rest for 20 minutes.

**Step 3**

Beat the cream cheese with an electric hand mixer on low speed until softened. Slowly beat in the honey and orange zest. Add the saffron mixture and continue to beat. Pour in the cream while continuing to beat on the lowest speed until the mixture is thick enough to firmly hold its shape. Spoon the mixture over the crust. Chill overnight.

**Nutrition Facts**

**Per Serving:**

458.7 calories; protein 4.6g 9% DV; carbohydrates 30.9g 10% DV; fat 35.8g 55% DV; cholesterol 108.9mg 36% DV; sodium 236mg 9% DV.

# Easy Cranberry Cheesecake

**Prep:** 15 mins **Cook:** 15 mins **Additional:** 1 hr **Total:** 1 hr 30 mins **Servings:** 8 **Yield:** 1 9-inch springform pan

### Ingredients

- ¾ cup graham cracker crumbs
- ½ cup chopped macadamia nuts
- ¼ cup melted margarine
- 2 tablespoons white sugar
- ¼ cup cold water
- 1 (.25 ounce) envelope unflavored gelatin

- 2 (8 ounce) packages cream cheese, softened
- 1 (7 ounce) jar marshmallow creme
- 1 (16 ounce) can whole berry cranberry sauce
- 1 cup frozen whipped topping (such as Cool Whip), thawed

### Directions

### Step 1

Preheat oven to 350 degrees F (175 degrees C).

### Step 2

Mix graham cracker crumbs, macadamia nuts, margarine, and sugar together in a bowl; press into the bottom of a 9-inch springform pan.

### Step 3

Bake in the preheated oven until crust is lightly browned, about 10 minutes. Cool crust.

### Step 4

Mix water and gelatin together in a saucepan over low heat until dissolved, 3 to 4 minutes.

### Step 5

Beat cream cheese and marshmallow cream together in a bowl using an electric mixer on medium speed until well mixed. Gradually stir gelatin mixture and cranberry sauce into cream cheese mixture; fold in whipped topping. Spoon mixture over crust. Chill cheesecake in the refrigerator until firm, at least 1 hour.

**Nutrition Facts**

**Per Serving:**

542.7 calories; protein 6.6g 13% DV; carbohydrates 54.2g 18% DV; fat 34.7g 53% DV; cholesterol 61.6mg 21% DV; sodium 315.4mg 13% DV.

# Churro Log Cabin

**Prep:** 1 hr **Total:** 1 hr **Servings:** 6 **Yield:** 1 log cabin

## Ingredients

- 1 (16 ounce) package canned white frosting
- 16 eaches pre-made churros (such as Tio Pepe's)
- 1 box toothpicks
- 7 cracker (2-1/2" square)s graham crackers
- 1 (14 ounce) package red licorice
- 1 cup gumdrops
- 1 cup small (2 1/2 inch tall) peppermint candy canes
- 1 (1.75 ounce) package holiday sprinkles
- 1 cup peppermint candies
- 2 cups shredded coconut
- ¼ cup confectioners' sugar

## Directions

### Step 1

Cabin Base: Fill a piping bag with frosting. Pipe a line of frosting along one side of a churro; lay frosting-side down on a serving platter. Repeat with 3 additional churros to form a square. Repeat with a second layer of churros, stacking them frosting side down on top of base layer. Repeat until walls are 4 churros high. Stick toothpicks vertically through churros at each corner for structural stability.

### Step 2

Roof: Center a graham cracker across the top of the cabin, using frosting to adhere it to the tops of the cabin walls. Lay a second graham cracker next to it; it will overhang the side of the cabin a bit. Adhere it with frosting. Repeat with a third graham cracker on the other side. Measure and cut 2 pieces of red licorice to the same length as the graham crackers, about 4x 3/4 inches; glue with frosting down the center of the middle graham cracker about 3 inches apart. These will hold up the A-frame roof. To form the A-frame, frost the long sides of 2 graham crackers and lean them together so top long sides meet and bottom long sides are set just inside the licorice lines. Decorate roof with licorice and gumdrops as desired.

### Step 3

Cabin Door: Break a graham cracker in half widthwise, spread a thin layer of frosting on one side, then decorate with candy canes and holiday sprinkles. Frost backside of door and stick it to the front of the log cabin.

**Step 4**

Windows: Break a graham cracker into quarters. Spread 3 quarters with a thin layer of frosting and decorate as desired. Frost backside of windows and stick them to sides and back of cabin.

**Step 5**

Icicles and Snow: Pipe frosting icicles along roofline, sprinkle coconut around cabin, and sift confectioners' sugar over the top.

**Nutrition Facts**

**Per Serving:**

1544.7 calories; protein 5.2g 10% DV; carbohydrates 280.9g 91% DV; fat 45.7g 70% DV; cholesterol 4.7mg 2% DV; sodium 370.3mg 15% DV.

# Cranberry Sweet Potato Spice Cake

**Prep:** 30 mins **Cook:** 1 hr 10 mins **Additional:** 10 mins **Total:** 1 hr 50 mins **Servings:** 16 **Yield:** 2 9-inch round cakes

**Ingredients**

- 3 cups all-purpose flour
- 2 teaspoons baking soda
- 2 teaspoons baking powder
- 2 teaspoons ground cinnamon
- 2 teaspoons ground nutmeg
- ½ teaspoon salt
- 1 ½ cups butter
- 1 ½ cups white sugar
- 3 large eggs eggs
- ½ cup molasses
- 1 tablespoon vanilla extract
- 3 cups cooked mashed sweet potatoes
- 1 ½ cups sweetened dried cranberries (such as Craisins)
- 1 cup chopped walnuts

**Directions**

**Step 1**

Preheat oven to 350 degrees F (175 degrees C). Grease and flour two 9-inch round baking pans.

**Step 2**

Sift flour, baking soda, baking powder, cinnamon, nutmeg, and salt together in a bowl.

## Step 3

Beat butter and sugar together in a separate large bowl with an electric mixer until light and fluffy. Beat one egg at a time into the butter mixture; add molasses and vanilla extract with last egg. Add sweet potatoes, cranberries, and walnuts; mix until batter is thoroughly combined. Gradually beat flour mixture into batter until thoroughly combined. Pour batter into prepared baking pans.

## Step 4

Bake in preheated oven until a toothpick inserted into the center comes out clean, about 1 hour 10 minutes. Cool in the pans for 10 minutes before turning out onto wire rack to cool completely.

## Nutrition Facts

## Per Serving:

493.2 calories; protein 5.9g 12% DV; carbohydrates 66.5g 22% DV; fat 23.6g 36% DV; cholesterol 80.6mg 27% DV; sodium 467.1mg 19% DV.

# Loving Loaf

**Servings:** 24 **Yield:** 2 - 8x4 inch loaf pans

## Ingredients

- ½ cup melted butter
- ⅓ cup white sugar
- 1 ½ cups crushed vanilla wafers
- 1 cup chopped pecans
- 1 cup butter, softened
- 2 cups white sugar

- 4 large eggs eggs
- 1 cup milk
- 2 teaspoons vanilla extract
- 2 ⅔ cups all-purpose flour
- 1 ½ teaspoons baking powder
- 1 teaspoon salt

## Directions

## Step 1

Preheat oven to 350 degrees F (175 degrees C). Grease two 8x4 inch bread pans.

## Step 2

Prepare the topping by combining the 1/2 cup butter, 1/3 cup sugar, vanilla wafers and pecans. Mix together well and press into the bottom of prepared pans.

## Step 3

Cream butter and sugar together. Add eggs one at a time and beat well. Combine milk and vanilla.

## Step 4

Sift flour, baking powder, and salt. Add to batter, alternating with milk; beat well. Pour into prepared loaf pans.

## Step 5

Bake in preheated oven at 350 degrees F (175 degrees C) for 1 hour, or until a toothpick inserted into the cake comes out clean. Remove from oven and cool on wire rack.

## Nutrition Facts

### Per Serving:

330.3 calories; protein 3.8g 8% DV; carbohydrates 39.3g 13% DV; fat 18.1g 28% DV; cholesterol 62.3mg 21% DV; sodium 259.7mg 10% DV.

# Frozen Christmas Pudding

**Servings:** 8 **Yield:** 8 servings

## Ingredients

- ½ cup raisins
- ½ cup sultana raisins
- ½ cup dried currants
- ¼ cup candied cherries, chopped
- ¼ cup candied mixed fruit peel
- ¼ cup fruit juice
- ¼ cup almonds
- 1 teaspoon ground cinnamon
- 1 teaspoon freshly grated nutmeg
- ½ cup heavy whipping cream
- 4 ¼ cups chocolate ice cream, softened

## Directions

### Step 1

In a medium bowl, combine fruit with fruit juice and spices. Cover, and allow to stand overnight.

### Step 2

The next day mix together soaked fruits, almonds, cream, and ice cream. Pour mixture into a large mold, and cover with foil. Freeze for at least one week to allow flavour to develop.

### Step 3

Unmold by quickly dipping into hot water, and inverting onto serving plate.

## Nutrition Facts

### Per Serving:

348.8 calories; protein 4.8g 10% DV; carbohydrates 52.3g 17% DV; fat 15.7g 24% DV; cholesterol 44.2mg 15% DV; sodium 69.6mg 3% DV.

# Chocolate-Stuffed Panettone

**Prep:** 30 mins **Cook:** 10 mins **Additional:** 15 mins **Total:** 55 mins **Servings:** 10 **Yield:** 10 servings

### Ingredients

- 2 (1 pound) loaves panettone

**Filling:**

- 11 ounces 70% dark chocolate, chopped
- 1 cup heavy whipping cream
- 1 tablespoon brandy
- ¾ cup chopped walnuts

**Glaze:**

- 1 (5 ounce) milk chocolate, chopped
- 1 tablespoon chopped dried apricots, or more to taste
- 1 tablespoon chopped walnuts, or more to taste

### Directions

#### Step 1

Slice off the top parts of the panettone right under the dome with a serrated knife. Cut into the panettone, leaving a 1/2-inch border around the edges and bottom and scoop out the soft interior. Crumble up the interior into a bowl.

#### Step 2

Place dark chocolate and cream in top of a double boiler over simmering water. Stir frequently, scraping down the sides with a rubber spatula to avoid scorching, until chocolate is melted, about 5 minutes. Remove from heat and stir in brandy. Fold in chopped walnuts and allow to cool for about 15 minutes. Combine chocolate mixture with panettone crumbs and mix well.

#### Step 3

Spoon chocolate-panettone mixture into the hollowed-out panettone. Hollow out and fill the lid if there's leftover filling. Cover stuffed panettone.

#### Step 4

Place milk chocolate in top of a double boiler over simmering water. Stir frequently, scraping down the sides with a rubber spatula to avoid scorching, until chocolate is melted, about 5 minutes. Drizzle melted chocolate over the top of the panettone and garnish with dried apricots and walnuts.

146

**Nutrition Facts**

**Per Serving:**

692.2 calories; protein 7.5g 15% DV; carbohydrates 85.9g 28% DV; fat 38g 58% DV; cholesterol 42.2mg 14% DV; sodium 268.2mg 11% DV.

# Easy Fruitcake Without Citron

**Servings:** 16 **Yield:** 1 - 10 x 14 inch tube cake

## Ingredients

- 3 cups dates, pitted and chopped
- 3 cups candied pineapple chunks
- 3 cups red and green candied cherries
- 8 cups walnut halves
- 2 cups all-purpose flour
- 2 teaspoons baking powder
- ½ teaspoon salt
- 4 large eggs eggs
- ½ cup dark corn syrup
- ¼ cup packed brown sugar
- ¼ cup vegetable oil

## Directions

### Step 1

Grease a 10 x 14 inch tube pan; line with waxed paper.

### Step 2

Mix fruits and nuts in a large bowl.

### Step 3

Sift dry ingredients in a separate bowl.

### Step 4

Mix eggs, corn syrup, sugar and oil in a medium size bowl. Gradually beat in dry ingredients. Pour over fruit mixture and mix. Firmly pack into pan.

### Step 5

Bake at 275 degrees F (135 degree C) about 2 hours and 15 minutes, or until top appears dry. Cool in pan.

**Nutrition Facts**

**Per Serving:**

689.2 calories; protein 11.5g 23% DV; carbohydrates 85.9g 28% DV; fat 37.5g 58% DV; cholesterol 46.5mg 16% DV; sodium 204mg 8% DV.

# Darling Husbands' Cake

**Servings:** 12 **Yield:** 1 - 9 inch square pan

## Ingredients

- ⅓ cup butter
- 1 cup white sugar
- 1 egg
- 2 cups all-purpose flour
- ¼ teaspoon salt
- 1 ½ teaspoons baking powder
- ½ cup chopped walnuts

- 1 teaspoon baking soda
- 1 teaspoon ground cinnamon
- 1 teaspoon ground allspice
- 1 teaspoon ground nutmeg
- 1 (10.75 ounce) can condensed tomato soup
- 1 cup chopped raisins

## Directions

### Step 1

Preheat oven to 350 degrees F (175 degrees C). Grease and flour a 9 inch square pan. Sift together flour, salt, baking powder, baking soda, cinnamon, allspice and nutmeg. Set aside.

### Step 2

Cream butter until it is soft and creamy. Add sugar and continue beating until light and fluffy. Add egg and beat well.

### Step 3

Add flour mixture and tomato soup. mix gently until blended, but don't overmix. Fold in nuts and raisins.

### Step 4

Spread batter into a 9 inch square pan. Bake at 350 degrees F (175 degrees C) for 55 to 60 minutes, or until toothpick inserted into cake comes out clean.

### Nutrition Facts

### Per Serving:

284.3 calories; protein 4.3g 9% DV; carbohydrates 48.1g 16% DV; fat 9.5g 15% DV; cholesterol 29.1mg 10% DV; sodium 399.4mg 16% DV.

# Pink Peppermint Cupcake

**Prep:** 10 mins **Cook:** 20 mins **Additional:** 30 mins **Total:** 1 hr **Servings:** 24 **Yield:** 24 cupcakes

## Ingredients

- 1 (18.25 ounce) package white cake mix
- 1 ⅓ cups water
- 3 large egg whites egg whites
- 2 tablespoons butter, melted
- ½ teaspoon peppermint extract
- 1 dash red food coloring, or as desired
- 1 (16 ounce) package vanilla frosting
- ½ cup crushed peppermint candies

## Directions

### Step 1

Preheat oven to 350 degrees F (175 degrees C). Line muffin cups with paper or aluminum foil liners.

### Step 2

Beat cake mix, water, egg whites, butter, peppermint extract, and food coloring together in a bowl using an electric mixer on low speed for 30 seconds. Increase speed to medium and continue to beat until smooth, scraping down sides as needed, about 2 minutes. Spoon batter into prepared muffin cups, filling about 3/4-full.

### Step 3

Bake in the preheated oven until a toothpick inserted in the center comes out clean, 20 to 22 minutes. Rotate tins halfway through the baking process to promote even baking. Transfer cupcakes to a wire rack to cool completely.

### Step 4

Frost cupcakes with vanilla frosting and top with crushed candies.

## Nutrition Facts

### Per Serving:

201.5 calories; protein 1.4g 3% DV; carbohydrates 34.6g 11% DV; fat 6.4g 10% DV; cholesterol 2.5mg 1% DV; sodium 192.9mg 8% DV.

# Mom's Christmas Plum Pudding

**Prep:** 15 mins **Cook:** 3 hrs 45 mins **Additional:** 30 mins **Total:** 4 hrs 30 mins **Servings:** 16 **Yield:** 16 servings

## Ingredients

### Pudding:

- 2 (15 ounce) cans purple plums - drained, pitted, and chopped
- 16 ounces gingersnaps, crushed
- 2 cups all-purpose flour
- 1 ½ cups white sugar
- ¾ cup milk

- ¾ cup melted butter
- 3 eaches eggs, beaten
- 1 tablespoon baking powder
- 1 teaspoon salt
- 1 teaspoon ground cinnamon
- ½ teaspoon ground nutmeg

### Brandy Sauce:

- 1 ½ cups white sugar
- ⅓ cup half-and-half
- 3 tablespoons butter

- 3 tablespoons brandy
- 3 tablespoons light corn syrup

## Directions

### Step 1

Generously grease a 12-cup steamed pudding mold and its lid.

### Step 2

Stir together plums, crushed gingersnaps, flour, sugar, milk, butter, eggs, baking powder, salt, cinnamon, and nutmeg for the pudding. Pour into the prepared pudding mold and cover with the lid. Place the mold on a rack in a deep, 8-quart pot. Add boiling water to halfway up the side of the mold, making sure water does not touch the lid.

### Step 3

Cover the pot and simmer for 3 hours 45 minutes, adding more boiling water, if necessary. Remove the pudding mold from the pot and cool on a wire rack until pudding pulls away from the side of the mold, about 30 minutes.

### Step 4

While pudding is cooling, combine sugar, half-and-half, butter, brandy, and corn syrup in a small, heavy saucepan. Cook over low heat, stirring occasionally, until butter melts, and sugar dissolves, 3 to 5 minutes.

**Step 5**

Invert pudding onto a platter and serve immediately alongside warm brandy sauce.

**Nutrition Facts**

**Per Serving:**

493.3 calories; protein 5.1g 10% DV; carbohydrates 84g 27% DV; fat 15.4g 24% DV; cholesterol 62.1mg 21% DV; sodium 530.5mg 21% DV.

# Grandma's Christmas Cupcakes

**Prep:** 1 hr **Cook:** 20 mins **Additional:** 30 mins **Total:** 1 hr 50 mins **Servings:** 16 **Yield:** 16 cupcakes

**Ingredients**

- 9 tablespoons butter, softened
- 1 cup superfine sugar
- 4 drops almond extract, or more to taste
- 4 large eggs eggs
- 1 cup self-rising flour
- 1 ¾ cups ground almonds

- round cookie or biscuit cutter
- small holly leaf-shaped cutter
- 1 pound ready-to-use white fondant, divided
- ¼ cup confectioners' sugar, or as needed
- 2 drops green food coloring, or as desired
- 1 drop red food coloring, or as needed

**Directions**

**Step 1**

Preheat oven to 350 degrees F (175 degrees C). Line 16 muffin cups with paper liners.

**Step 2**

Beat the butter, sugar, and almond extract in a mixing bowl with an electric mixer until light and fluffy. Beat in the eggs one at a time, mixing well after each addition, followed by the self-rising flour. Gently fold the ground almonds into the batter; spoon batter into the prepared cupcake cups, filling them about halfway.

**Step 3**

Bake the cupcakes until they have risen and a toothpick inserted into the center of a cupcake comes out clean, about 20 minutes. Allow the cupcakes to cool completely.

**Step 4**

To decorate, knead the fondant until pliable; set aside about 1/3 of the fondant. Roll out the larger portion of the fondant on a work surface dusted generously with confectioners' sugar. Using a round cookie or biscuit cutter the same size as the cupcake tops, cut out circles of the fondant; place a fondant circle on each cupcake. Press the fondant down lightly.

### Step 5

Divide the remaining fondant into four even portions; place 3 portions into a bowl and the other into a second small bowl. Tint the larger portion to your desired shade of green with the green food coloring. Tint the smaller portion to your desired shade of red food coloring.

### Step 6

Roll out the green fondant on a work surface generously dusted with confectioners' sugar and cut out 32 holly leaves with leaf-shaped cutter. Use your finger to rub away any white confectioners' sugar on the green leaves and arrange 2 leaves on each cupcake. Roll red fondant into 48 small red berries and place 3 berries on the leaves of each cupcake.

### Nutrition Facts

### Per Serving:

323.2 calories; protein 7.3g 15% DV; carbohydrates 48.2g 16% DV; fat 11.7g 18% DV; cholesterol 63.7mg 21% DV; sodium 163.7mg 7% DV.

# Santa Hat Cupcakes

**Prep:** 45 mins **Total:** 45 mins **Servings:** 12 **Yield:** 12 cupcakes

### Ingredients

- 1 (16 ounce) package vanilla frosting, divided
- 12 eaches unfrosted cupcakes, cooled
- ¼ cup red colored sugar or sprinkles
- 4 eaches fresh strawberries, hulled

- 3 ounces ready-to-use white fondant
- 2 drops red food coloring, or as needed
- 2 tablespoons confectioners' sugar, or as needed

### Directions

### Step 1

For the Santa hat cupcakes with sprinkles: Place some of the frosting into a piping bag with a large round tip. Pipe frosting perpendicularly to the center of the cupcake in the shape of a Santa hat, using gradually less pressure to create a cone shape. Cover cone with red colored sugar or red sprinkles. Spoon some frosting into a piping bag with a small star-shaped tip. Pipe frosting around the base of the hat for the rim and pipe a small pom-pom on top. Repeat with 3 more cupcakes.

### Step 2

For the Santa hat cupcakes with strawberries: Frost 4 cupcakes with a thin layer of vanilla frosting. Place a strawberry in the center, with the tip facing up. Pipe a small pom-pom on top of the strawberry using the small star-shaped tip. Pipe frosting around the base of the cupcake using the large round tip to create the hat's rim. Create swirls in the rim with a finger. Repeat with remaining 3 frosted cupcakes.

## Step 3

For the Santa hat cupcakes with fondant: Color white fondant with red food coloring. Sprinkle a work surface with confectioners' sugar and roll out 1/4 of the fondant into a very thin 2 1/2-inch circle. Cut a wedge from the circle, leaving a Pac-Man shape. Use the large round tip to pipe a cone of frosting in the center of each cupcake. Fold the cut edges of the fondant together to create a cone shape and place red fondant hat around the frosting cone. Use the star-shaped tip to pipe frosting around the base for the rim and a small pom-pom on top. Repeat with 3 more cupcakes.

## Nutrition Facts

### Per Serving:

334.9 calories; protein 1.8g 4% DV; carbohydrates 56.1g 18% DV; fat 11.6g 18% DV; cholesterol 18.4mg 6% DV; sodium 187.6mg 8% DV.

# Mint Devil's Food Cupcakes

**Prep:** 35 mins **Cook:** 35 mins **Additional:** 55 mins **Total:** 2 hrs 5 mins **Servings:** 12 **Yield:** 1 dozen cupcakes

## Ingredients

### Cupcakes:

- cooking spray
- ¼ cup unsalted butter
- 2 (1 ounce) squares semisweet chocolate
- 1 cup all-purpose flour
- 2 tablespoons all-purpose flour
- ¾ teaspoon baking soda
- ⅛ teaspoon salt
- 2 tablespoons milk
- ½ teaspoon distilled white vinegar
- ½ drop pure peppermint extract
- 1 cup white sugar
- 1 egg
- ½ cup boiling water

### Whipped Cream Frosting:

- 2 tablespoons cold water, or more as needed
- 1 (.25 ounce) package unflavored gelatin
- 1 cup heavy whipping cream
- 3 tablespoons heavy whipping cream
- ¼ cup confectioners' sugar
- 2 teaspoons confectioners' sugar
- ½ teaspoon imitation vanilla extract
- 1 drop green food coloring
- 6 cookies chocolate sandwich cookies (such as Oreo)

153

## Directions

### Step 1

Preheat oven to 350 degrees F (175 degrees C). Lightly spray 12 muffin cups.

### Step 2

Heat butter and chocolate together in a small saucepan over low heat until melted, about 5 minutes. Remove from heat; set aside to cool slightly, about 5 minutes.

### Step 3

Combine 1 cup plus 2 tablespoons flour, baking soda, and salt together in a small bowl.

### Step 4

Mix milk, vinegar, and peppermint extract together in another small bowl.

### Step 5

Beat sugar and eggs together in large bowl with an electric mixer on medium speed until pale, about 3 minutes. Add melted chocolate and beat well to combine. Pour in 1/2 cup boiling water and beat until batter is well-blended. Add flour mixture; beat on low speed until incorporated. Add milk mixture and blend well. Fill muffin cups 3/4-full with batter.

### Step 6

Bake in the preheated oven until a toothpick inserted into a cupcake comes out clean, 25 to 30 minutes. Transfer cupcakes to wire rack and cool to room temperature, about 45 minutes.

### Step 7

Combine 2 tablespoons cold water and gelatin in a small saucepan over low heat. Stir constantly until gelatin dissolves, about 5 minutes. Remove from heat and let cool slightly, but not until set, about 5 minutes.

### Step 8

Combine 1 cup plus 3 tablespoons heavy cream, 1/4 cup plus 2 teaspoons confectioners' sugar, vanilla extract, and green food coloring in a large bowl. Whip with an electric mixer on low speed until slightly thickened, about 5 minutes. Beat in dissolved gelatin slowly. Increase speed to high and beat until frosting is stiff, about 3 minutes.

### Step 9

Spread frosting over cooled cupcakes. Remove and discard cream filling from chocolate sandwich cookies; crush cookies. Scatter cookie crumbs over cupcakes.

# Sausage Christmas Cake

**Servings:** 12 **Yield:** 10 -15 servings

## Ingredients

- 1 pound pork sausage
- 1 cup cold, brewed coffee
- 1 cup packed dark brown sugar
- 1 cup white sugar
- 2 large eggs eggs, beaten
- 1 teaspoon ground cinnamon
- 1 teaspoon ground nutmeg
- ½ teaspoon ground cloves
- 2 cups self-rising flour
- 1 cup chopped walnuts
- ½ cup golden raisins
- ½ cup raisins

## Directions

### Step 1

Mix together cinnamon, nutmeg, cloves, and flour in a bowl.

### Step 2

Add sausage, coffee, sugars, and eggs to the dry ingredients. Add raisins and nuts. Pour into an ungreased angel food cake pan.

### Step 3

Bake in preheated oven at 350 degrees F (175 degrees C) for 1 hour or till a toothpick comes out clean.

### Step 4

Garnishes may be added such as drizzled white frosting with whole cherries and mint leaves. This cake is so moist. If you like the flavor of rum you can wrap a rum-soaked damp cloth around it and refrigerate for several weeks. Best served with a spoonful of whipped cream.

**Nutrition Facts**

**Per Serving:**

479.9 calories; protein 9.5g 19% DV; carbohydrates 61.8g 20% DV; fat 22.8g 35% DV; cholesterol 56.7mg 19% DV; sodium 536mg 21% DV.

# Eggnog-Chai Cupcakes

**Prep:** 20 mins **Cook:** 22 mins **Additional:** 5 mins **Total:** 47 mins **Servings:** 12 **Yield:** 1 dozen cupcakes

## Ingredients

### Cupcakes:

- 1 (15.25 ounce) package spiced cake mix (such as Betty Crocker)
- 1 cup brewed chai tea
- ½ cup vegetable oil
- 3 large eggs eggs

### Frosting:

- ½ cup butter, softened
- 1 (8 ounce) package cream cheese, softened
- 2 cups confectioners' sugar
- 1 teaspoon vanilla extract
- ½ teaspoon ground nutmeg
- 2 tablespoons eggnog
- 1 teaspoon rum extract

## Directions

### Step 1

Preheat oven to 350 degrees F (175 degrees C). Line muffin cups with paper liners.

### Step 2

Beat cake mix, chai tea, vegetable oil, and eggs together in a bowl using an electric mixer on low speed for 30 seconds. Increase speed to medium and beat until batter is smooth, about 2 minutes more. Spoon batter into the prepared muffin cups, filling 2/3-full.

### Step 3

Bake in the preheated oven until a toothpick inserted in the center comes out clean, 22 to 24 minutes. Cool cupcakes in the tin for 5 minutes before transferring to a wire rack to cool completely.

### Step 4

Beat butter and cream cheese together in a bowl using an electric mixer on medium speed until smooth, 20 to 30 seconds. Add confectioners' sugar, vanilla extract, and nutmeg and beat on medium-high speed until smooth, about 1 minute. Scrape sides of bowl as needed. Add eggnog and beat until fully incorporated into the frosting; beat in rum extract on medium-low speed.

### Step 5

Transfer frosting to a pastry bag or plastic bag with a corner snipped and pipe frosting onto cooled cupcakes.

# Elegant Easy Torte

**Prep:** 15 mins **Total:** 15 mins **Servings:** 8 **Yield:** 8 servings

## Ingredients

- 1 (13 ounce) package frozen pound cake, thawed
- 1 (12.5 ounce) can cherry pie filling, or flavor of choice
- 8 ounces whipped topping
- ½ cup chopped nuts

## Directions

### Step 1

Slice thawed pound cake horizontally into 3 layers. Spread bottom layer with pie filling, and top with center slice. Spread middle layer with whipped topping, and cover with last slice. Sprinkle with chopped nuts.

### Step 2

Slice, and serve. Store in the refrigerator.

**Nutrition Facts**

**Per Serving:**

373.8 calories; protein 4.5g 9% DV; carbohydrates 43.3g 14% DV; fat 21.3g 33% DV; cholesterol 101.9mg 34% DV; sodium 199.5mg 8% DV.

# Triple Eggnog Cake

**Prep:** 20 mins **Cook:** 30 mins **Additional:** 1 hr **Total:** 1 hr 50 mins **Servings:** 15 **Yield:** 1 cake

## Ingredients

**Cake:**

- 1 (15.25 ounce) package yellow cake mix
- 1 ½ cups eggnog, or more to taste
- 2 large eggs eggs
- ¼ cup melted butter

- ½ teaspoon ground nutmeg
- ½ teaspoon rum-flavored extract

**Filling:**

- 2 cups eggnog
- 1 (3.5 ounce) package instant vanilla pudding mix
- ½ teaspoon rum-flavored extract

**Topping:**

- 2 tablespoons cold water
- 1 tablespoon unflavored gelatin
- 2 cups heavy whipping cream
- 1 ¼ cups white sugar
- ½ teaspoon rum-flavored extract
- 1 pinch salt

**Directions**

**Step 1**

Preheat oven to 350 degrees F (175 degrees C). Grease 2 round cake pans.

**Step 2**

Mix cake mix, 1 1/2 cups eggnog, eggs, butter, nutmeg, and 1/2 teaspoon rum-flavored extract together in a bowl using an electric mixer until batter is smooth, about 4 minutes. Pour batter into the prepared pans.

**Step 3**

Bake in the preheated oven until a toothpick inserted in the center comes out clean, about 30 minutes. Remove cakes from pans and cool on a wire rack.

**Step 4**

Mix 2 cups eggnog, vanilla pudding mix, and 1/2 teaspoon rum-flavored extract together in a bowl until smooth; refrigerate until pudding thickens, at least 30 minutes.

**Step 5**

Mix cold water and gelatin together in a bowl until gelatin is dissolved. Beat cream in a separate bowl using an electric mixer until soft peaks form; add gelatin mixture, white sugar, 1/2 teaspoon rum-flavored extract, and salt and beat until stiff peaks form. Refrigerate topping until chilled, at least 30 minutes.

**Step 6**

Place 1 cake on a serving plate and spread 1/2 of the filling on top. Place the second cake over the filling and top with remaining filling. Cover entire cake with whipped cream topping. Store cake in refrigerator.

**Per Serving:**

440.6 calories; protein 5.1g 10% DV; carbohydrates 54.2g 18% DV; fat 23.3g 36% DV; cholesterol 112mg 37% DV; sodium 369mg 15% DV.

# Christmas Tree Mini Cupcakes

**Prep:** 30 mins **Cook:** 8 mins **Additional:** 10 mins **Total:** 48 mins **Servings:** 48 **Yield:** 4 dozen mini cupcakes

## Ingredients

### Cupcakes:

- 1 ½ cups pastry flour
- 1 cup white sugar
- ⅓ cup cocoa powder

- 1 cup water
- ½ cup vegetable oil
- 1 teaspoon vanilla extract

### Toppings:

- 1 cup vanilla frosting, or as desired
- 1 drop green food coloring, or as desired
- 48 small strawberries, hulled

- ¼ cup round red candies, or as desired
- star-shaped candies

## Directions

### Step 1

Preheat oven to 350 degrees F (175 degrees C). Grease mini muffin cups or line with paper liners.

### Step 2

Mix pastry flour, white sugar, and cocoa powder together in a bowl; add water, oil, and vanilla extract and blend until batter is smooth. Spoon batter into the prepared muffin cups.

### Step 3

Bake in the preheated oven until a toothpick inserted in the center comes out clean, 8 to 12 minutes. Cool in the tin for 5 minutes.

### Step 4

Mix frosting and green food coloring together in a bowl until evenly combined. Transfer frosting to a pipe bag or plastic bag with a snipped corner; refrigerate for 5 minutes.

### Step 5

Squeeze a small amount of frosting onto the hulled side of each strawberry and place each onto a cupcake so the strawberry is in the shape of a tree. Pipe frosting onto each strawberry to look like leaves. Add candies to the "tree" to look like ornaments and place a star-shaped candy on top of each "tree".

**Nutrition Facts**

**Per Serving:**

76.5 calories; protein 0.5g 1% DV; carbohydrates 12.2g 4% DV; fat 3.2g 5% DV; cholesterolmg; sodium 9.4mg.

# No-Bake Raisin Cheesecake

**Servings:** 12 **Yield:** 1 - 8 inch cheesecake

## Ingredients

- ¼ cup golden raisins
- ¼ cup raisins
- 1 cup plain low-fat yogurt
- 1 (3 ounce) package cream cheese
- 1 ¼ cups low-fat cottage cheese
- 1 teaspoon vanilla extract

- ½ cup white sugar
- ½ cup low-fat milk
- 1 (.25 ounce) package unflavored gelatin
- 3 large egg whites egg whites
- 1 cup boiling water
- 2 tablespoons water

## Directions

### Step 1

Put all the raisins in a small bowl, and pour hot water over them. Set the bowl aside.

### Step 2

Heat 1/4 cup white sugar with 2 tablespoons water in a small saucepan over medium-high heat. Boil the mixture until the bubbles rise to the surface in a random pattern. This indicates that the water has nearly evaporated, and that the sugar is beginning to cook. With a small spoon, drop a bit of the sugar into a bowl filled with ice water. If the sugar dissolves immediately, continue cooking the sugar mixture. Remove from heat when the sugar dropped into the water can be rolled between your fingers into a ball.

### Step 3

Begin beating the egg whites with an electric mixer on high speed. Pour the sugar syrup down the side of the bowl in a thin, steady stream. When all the sugar has been incorporated, decrease mixer speed to medium. Continue beating until the egg whites are glossy, have formed stiff peaks, and have cooled to room temperature--about 10 minutes. Increase the speed to high, and beat the meringue for 1 minute more.

### Step 4

Puree the yogurt, cream cheese, cottage cheese, vanilla extract, and 1/4 cup white sugar in a food processor or blender. Scrape the cheese mixture into a large bowl.

### Step 5

Pour the milk into a small saucepan. Sprinkle the gelatin over the milk. Let it stand until the gelatin softens, about 5 minutes. Heat the milk over a medium heat, stirring until the gelatin is dissolved. Stir the milk into the cheese mixture. Mix about 1/3 of the meringue into the cheese mixture to lighten it. Gently fold in the rest of the meringue.

### Step 6

Line an 8 inch cake pan with plastic wrap. Drain the raisins, and scatter them in the bottom of the pan. Then pour the cheesecake batter into the lined pan. Chill for 4 hours. To turn out the cheesecake, invert a serving plate on top of the pan. Turn both over together. Lift away the pan, peel off the plastic wrap, and slice for serving.

**Nutrition Facts**

**Per Serving:**

121.3 calories; protein 6.8g 14% DV; carbohydrates 16.2g 5% DV; fat 3.5g 5% DV; cholesterol 11.7mg 4% DV; sodium 151.4mg 6% DV.

# Carrot Pudding

**Servings: 8 Yield:** 8 servings

## Ingredients

- ½ cup butter
- 1 cup white sugar
- 1 tablespoon minced carrot
- 1 cup peeled and shredded potatoes
- 1 cup all-purpose flour
- 2 cups raisins
- salt to taste
- 1 teaspoon ground cinnamon

- ¼ teaspoon ground nutmeg
- 1 teaspoon baking soda
- ½ cup green apples
- ½ cup white sugar
- 1 ½ tablespoons cornstarch
- 1 cup water
- 2 tablespoons butter
- 1 ½ tablespoons lemon juice

## Directions

### Step 1

Cream 1/2 cup butter or margarine and 1 cup sugar. Mix in carrots, potatoes, and raisins. Sift flour, baking soda, salt, and spices together; mix into the creamed mixture. Stir in apples.

**Step 2**

Fill cans 2/3 full with pudding mixture. Cover with foil.

**Step 3**

Place cans in a roasting pan with 2 to 3 inches of water. Steam at 300 degrees F (150 degrees C) for 2 1/2 to 3 hours.

**Step 4**

Stir together 1/2 cup sugar and cornstarch. Combine mixture with water in a saucepan. Cook and stir over low heat until thick. Stir in 2 tablespoons butter or margarine and lemon juice. Serve warm over pudding.

**Nutrition Facts**

**Per Serving:**

464.5 calories; protein 3.3g 7% DV; carbohydrates 84.6g 27% DV; fat 14.8g 23% DV; cholesterol 38.1mg 13% DV; sodium 265.9mg 11% DV.

# Steamed Currant Cake

**Prep:** 20 mins **Cook:** 3 hrs **Total:** 3 hrs 20 mins **Servings:** 12 **Yield:** 1 - 9x5 inch loaf pan

**Ingredients**

- ¾ cup all-purpose flour
- ½ teaspoon ground cinnamon
- ½ teaspoon ground nutmeg
- 1 teaspoon baking soda
- ½ teaspoon salt
- 1 cup lard
- ¾ cup white sugar
- 2 large eggs eggs, beaten
- 1 cup chopped walnuts
- ⅔ cup chopped raisins
- ⅔ cup dried currants
- ⅔ cup chopped dates
- 1 cup fresh bread crumbs
- ½ cup orange juice
- 2 tablespoons butter
- ¾ cup confectioners' sugar
- ⅛ cup boiling water
- ⅛ cup brandy

**Directions**

**Step 1**

Grease and flour a 9x5 inch loaf pan and line bottom with parchment paper. Sift together the flour, cinnamon, nutmeg, baking soda and salt. Set aside. Place a rack in the bottom of a large pot, over medium heat, and fill to the top of the rack with boiling water.

## Step 2

In a large bowl cream the lard and sugar until fluffy. Beat in the eggs. Mix in the walnuts, chopped raisins, currants, dates, bread crumbs, and orange juice. Stir in the flour mixture until smooth. Pour into prepared pan.

## Step 3

Cover the top with 2 layers of parchment paper and tie down with string. Place the pan on the rack. Cover pot and steam cake for 3 hours. Make sure to add water as it evaporates. Serve warm with Hard Sauce.

## Step 4

To make the Hard Sauce: In a saucepan cream 2 tablespoons butter and 3/4 cup confectioners' sugar. Add 1/8 cup boiling water and 1/8 cup brandy. Cook, stirring, until clear and pour over individual servings.

**Nutrition Facts**

**Per Serving:**

430.4 calories; protein 4.3g 9% DV; carbohydrates 44.9g 15% DV; fat 26.6g 41% DV; cholesterol 52.3mg 17% DV; sodium 254.4mg 10% DV.

# Chocolate-Peppermint Roll

**Prep:** 15 mins **Cook:** 25 mins **Additional:** 5 mins **Total:** 45 mins **Servings:** 12 **Yield:** 1 roll

### Ingredients

- 5 large egg whites egg whites
- 1 cup white sugar, divided
- 5 large egg yolks egg yolks
- ¼ teaspoon salt

- ¾ cup all-purpose flour
- ¼ cup cocoa powder
- ⅛ cup powdered sugar, or as needed
- 1 ½ pints peppermint ice cream

### Directions

### Step 1

Preheat the oven to 350 degrees F (175 degrees C). Line a shallow 11x5-inch baking pan with greased waxed paper.

**Step 2**

Beat egg whites using an electric mixer in a mixing bowl until light and fluffy. Gradually add 1/2 cup white sugar and beat until combined.

**Step 3**

Beat egg yolks and salt together using an electric mixer in a separate bowl until light and fluffy. Gradually add remaining 1/2 cup sugar and beat until combined. Fold in egg white mixture. Fold in flour and cocoa powder. Pour batter into the prepared pan.

**Step 4**

Bake in the preheated oven until a toothpick inserted into the center comes out clean, about 25 minutes.

**Step 5**

Remove from the oven and turn cake onto a towel sprinkled heavily with powdered sugar. Remove waxed paper from cake and form into a roll. Let stand for about 4 minutes.

**Step 6**

Unroll cake and spread evenly with peppermint ice cream. Re-roll and freeze until ready to serve.

**Nutrition Facts**

**Per Serving:**

196.9 calories; protein 4.9g 10% DV; carbohydrates 33g 11% DV; fat 5.8g 9% DV; cholesterol 99.9mg 33% DV; sodium 101.8mg 4% DV.

# Best Christmas Cranberry Torte

**Prep:** 30 mins **Cook:** 10 mins **Additional:** 8 hrs 30 mins **Total:** 9 hrs 10 mins **Servings:** 8 **Yield:** 1 8-inch torte

**Ingredients**

**Graham Cracker Crust:**

- 1 ½ cups graham cracker crumbs
- ½ cup chopped pecans
- ¼ cup white sugar
- 6 tablespoons butter, melted

**Filling:**

- 2 cups fresh cranberries, ground
- 1 cup white sugar
- 2 large egg whites pasteurized egg whites
- 1 tablespoon frozen orange juice concentrate, thawed
- 1 teaspoon vanilla extract

164

- ⅛ teaspoon salt

**Cranberry Glaze:**

- ½ cup white sugar
- 1 tablespoon cornstarch
- ¾ cup fresh cranberries

- 1 cup whipping cream

- ⅔ cup water
- 1 orange, sliced, or as needed

**Directions**

**Step 1**

Combine graham cracker crumbs, pecans, sugar, and butter in a mixing bowl for crust. Press into the bottom and up the sides of an 8-inch springform pan. Chill.

**Step 2**

Meanwhile, combine cranberries and sugar for filling in a large mixing bowl. Let stand for 5 minutes. Add egg whites, orange juice, vanilla extract, and salt. Beat using an electric mixer on low speed until frothy. Beat on high until stiff peaks form (when the tips stand straight), 6 to 8 minutes.

**Step 3**

Whip cream in a small mixing bowl until soft peaks (or until the tips curl over); fold into cranberry mixture. Turn into crust and freeze until firm, 8 hours to overnight.

**Step 4**

Stir sugar and cornstarch for glaze together in a saucepan. Stir in cranberries and water. Cook and stir over medium-low heat until bubbly, about 5 minutes. Continue to cook, stirring occasionally, just until cranberry skins pop, about 5 minutes. Let cool to room temperature, about 30 minutes; do not chill.

**Step 5**

Remove torte from the pan. Place on a serving plate. Spoon cranberry glaze in the center; place orange slices around the outside.

**Nutrition Facts**

**Per Serving:**

493.7 calories; protein 3.6g 7% DV; carbohydrates 64.5g 21% DV; fat 26.2g 40% DV; cholesterol 63.7mg 21% DV; sodium 219.7mg 9% DV.

# Pousse Café

**Servings:** 12 **Yield:** 1 fluted 2 quart ring mold

## Ingredients

- 2 ¼ cups pastry flour
- ½ teaspoon salt
- 2 ½ teaspoons baking powder
- ¾ cup shortening
- 1 ½ cups white sugar
- 3 large eggs eggs
- 1 teaspoon vanilla extract
- 3 tablespoons cognac
- ½ cup milk
- ½ cup light cream
- 2 cups heavy whipping cream
- ¼ cup white sugar
- 1 teaspoon instant coffee granules
- 1 tablespoon cognac

## Directions

### Step 1

Preheat oven to 350 degrees F (175 degrees C). Grease thoroughly a fluted 2 quart ring mold, and dust lightly with flour.

### Step 2

Sift pastry flour, salt, and baking powder together.

### Step 3

In a large bowl, cream shortening well. Gradually blend in 1 1/2 cups sugar, eggs, vanilla, and 3 tablespoons cognac; beat until light and fluffy. Gently blend sifted ingredients alternately with the milk and cream into the creamed mixture. Pour batter into ring mold.

### Step 4

Bake for 45 to 50 minutes, or until cake springs back when lightly touched. Remove from pan, and allow to cool.

### Step 5

In a clean, cold bowl, beat the 2 cups whipping cream until peaks form. Stir in 1/4 cup sugar and coffee powder. Frost the cake with whipped cream. When serving, drizzle cake with a few drops of cognac.

## Nutrition Facts

### Per Serving:

500.5 calories; protein 5.2g 11% DV; carbohydrates 48.8g 16% DV; fat 31.2g 48% DV; cholesterol 108.3mg 36% DV; sodium 239.3mg 10% DV.

# Pumpkin Spice Ring

**Servings:** 10 **Yield:** 10 servings

## Ingredients

- 1 (18.25 ounce) package angel food cake mix
- 1 cup pumpkin puree
- ½ teaspoon pumpkin pie spice

## Directions

### Step 1

Combine pumpkin and pumpkin pie spice, and mix well. Set aside.

### Step 2

Mix cake as directed on package. Fold in pumpkin mixture. Pour into an ungreased tube pan.

### Step 3

Bake at 350 degrees F (175 degrees C) until lightly browned, using the box directions as a guide to cooking time.

### Nutrition Facts

### Per Serving:

196.9 calories; protein 4.3g 9% DV; carbohydrates 43.7g 14% DV; fat 0.1g; cholesterolmg; sodium 502.9mg 20% DV.

# Hot Milk Sponge Cake

**Prep:** 15 mins **Cook:** 50 mins **Total:** 1 hr 5 mins **Servings:** 12 **Yield:** 1 large loaf cake

## Ingredients

- ¾ cup milk
- 2 tablespoons butter
- 3 large eggs eggs
- 1 ½ cups white sugar
- 1 ½ cups all-purpose flour
- 1 ½ teaspoons baking powder
- 1 teaspoon vanilla extract

## Directions

### Step 1

Preheat oven to 350 degrees F (175 degrees C). Grease one large loaf pan or one 10 inch tube pan.

**Step 2**

In a saucepan over medium-low heat, combine the milk and the butter. Do not boil.

**Step 3**

In a large bowl beat the eggs until light colored. Gradually add the sugar to the eggs then stir in the flour and baking powder. Stir in the hot milk and butter. Beat only until combined. Stir in the vanilla. Pour the batter into the prepared pan.

**Step 4**

Bake at 350 degrees F (175 degrees C) for 45 to 50 minutes. Let cake cool in pan for 10 minutes. Remove cake from the pan and cool on a wire rack.

**Nutrition Facts**

**Per Serving:**

197.4 calories; protein 3.7g 7% DV; carbohydrates 37.9g 12% DV; fat 3.6g 6% DV; cholesterol 52.8mg 18% DV; sodium 98.7mg 4% DV.

# Apricot Fruitcake

**Servings: 24 Yield:** 2 - 9 inch tube pans

## Ingredients

- 1 cup dried apricots
- 1 cup water
- ¾ cup butter
- 1 cup white sugar
- 4 large eggs eggs
- 1 cup golden raisins
- 1 pound red and green candied cherries
- 6 piece (blank)s candied pineapple slices
- 1 pound dried mixed fruit
- 2 cups all-purpose flour, divided
- ½ teaspoon baking soda
- ½ teaspoon salt
- ½ cup apricot nectar
- 1 cup chopped walnuts

## Directions

**Step 1**

Preheat oven to 275 degrees F (135 degrees C). Grease two 9 inch tube pans.

**Step 2**

In a saucepan over medium heat cook apricots in the water until they are mushy. Press them through a sieve and let them cool.

## Step 3

Separate the eggs. Beat the egg yolks until lemony colored. Then beat the egg whites until stiff peaks are formed. Set aside.

## Step 4

Cream the butter or margarine and sugar together. Add the beaten egg yolks and the apricots, and mix thoroughly.

## Step 5

Combine the raisins, candied cherries, candied pineapple, and mixed dried fruits in a bowl coated with one cup of the flour.

## Step 6

Combine the remaining flour, baking soda, and salt. Add this flour mixture alternately to the creamed mixture with the apricot juice. Blend this batter into the mixed fruits. Add the chopped pecans or walnuts and fold in the beaten egg whites. Turn the batter into the prepared pans.

## Step 7

Bake at 275 degrees F (135 degrees C) for 2 hours. Garnish cakes with candied pineapples and cherries. Makes about 24 servings.

### Nutrition Facts

### Per Serving:

296.3 calories; protein 3.8g 8% DV; carbohydrates 51g 16% DV; fat 10g 15% DV; cholesterol 46.3mg 15% DV; sodium 145.2mg 6% DV.

# Christmas Cherry Cake

**Servings:** 24 **Yield:** 1 9 x 5-inch loaf

### Ingredients

- 1 cup white sugar
- 1 cup butter
- 2 large eggs eggs
- ½ cup orange juice
- 2 cups all-purpose flour
- 1 teaspoon baking powder
- 12 ounces golden raisins
- 8 ounces halved glace cherries

### Directions

### Step 1

Preheat oven to 300 degrees F (150 degrees C). Grease and line with parchment paper one 9x5 inch loaf pan.

**Step 2**

Cream butter or margarine and sugar together until light and fluffy. Add beaten eggs and orange juice and mix well.

**Step 3**

Sift flour and baking powder. Reserve 1/3 cup of flour mixture and toss with raisins and cherries (this will keep them from sinking to the bottom of the cake). Add flour mixture to batter and blend. Add floured raisins and cherries to dough and mix until just combined. Pour batter into prepared pan.

**Step 4**

Bake at 300 degrees F (150 degrees C) for 2-1/2 hours. Don't serve until several days old. Wrap the cake in plastic wrap or foil and store in a sealed tin.

**Nutrition Facts**

**Per Serving:**

205.1 calories; protein 2g 4% DV; carbohydrates 32.5g 11% DV; fat 8.3g 13% DV; cholesterol 35.8mg 12% DV; sodium 94.1mg 4% DV.

# Orange Crunch Bundt Cake

**Servings:** 16 **Yield:** 1 - 10 inch bundt cake

**Ingredients**

- 1 cup butter
- 1 cup white sugar
- 2 large eggs eggs
- 1 cup sour cream
- 2 cups all-purpose flour
- 1 teaspoon baking soda

- 1 cup raisins
- ½ cup walnuts
- 1 teaspoon vanilla extract
- 2 tablespoons orange zest
- ¼ cup orange juice
- ½ cup white sugar

**Directions**

**Step 1**

Preheat oven to 350 degrees F (175 degrees C). Grease and flour a 10 inch bundt pan.

**Step 2**

Cream butter or margarine and 1 cup sugar. Add eggs, and beat well with an electric mixer at medium speed. Mix in sour cream and vanilla. Combine flour and baking soda: add to creamed mixture, blending just until moistened. Stir in raisins, walnuts, and orange rind. Mix well. Pour batter into prepared pan.

### Step 3

Bake for 60 minutes, or until a wooden pick comes out clean. Cool cake in pan for 5 minutes.

### Step 4

Dissolve 1/2 cup sugar in orange juice. Pour over hot cake. Cool completely in pan.

### Nutrition Facts

### Per Serving:

321.6 calories; protein 3.8g 8% DV; carbohydrates 39.6g 13% DV; fat 17.4g 27% DV; cholesterol 60.1mg 20% DV; sodium 178.2mg 7% DV.

# Christmas Cheese Cake

**Servings:** 11 **Yield:** 10 - 12 servings

### Ingredients

- 1 (3 ounce) package ladyfinger cookies
- 3 (8 ounce) packages cream cheese
- 1 cup white sugar
- 4 large eggs eggs
- 1 ½ pints sour cream
- 1 tablespoon vanilla extract
- 1 tablespoon almond extract
- 1 (21 ounce) can cherry pie filling

### Directions

### Step 1

Preheat oven to 375 degrees F (190 degrees C). Line the sides of one 10 inch springform pan with lady fingers then line the bottom with lady fingers (cutting lady fingers, if necessary).

### Step 2

Cream the cream cheese and sugar together. Add the eggs, one at a time, beating after each addition. Stir in the extracts and fold in the sour cream. Pour batter into the prepared pan. Cover tops of lady fingers with foil.

### Step 3

Bake at 375 degrees F (190 degrees C) for 50 to 60 minutes, until almost set in the middle. Remove cake from oven and let stand for 1/2 hour, then remove sides of pan. Place in the refrigerator for at least 24 hours. Before serving top with canned pie filling.

**Nutrition Facts**

**Per Serving:**

540.6 calories; protein 9.9g 20% DV; carbohydrates 42.5g 14% DV; fat 37g 57% DV; cholesterol 179.3mg 60% DV; sodium 260.6mg 10% DV.

# Carrot-Oatmeal Spice Cake

**Servings: 15 Yield: 1 - 7x11 inch pan**

## Ingredients

- 1 cup raisins
- ⅓ cup shredded carrots
- 2 cups water
- 1 cup all-purpose flour
- 1 cup quick cooking oats
- 1 ½ teaspoons artificial sweetener
- ½ teaspoon salt

- 1 teaspoon baking soda
- 1 teaspoon ground cinnamon
- ½ cup margarine, softened
- ¼ cup egg substitute
- 1 teaspoon vanilla extract
- ⅓ cup pecans, coarsely chopped

## Directions

### Step 1

Preheat oven to 350 degrees F (175 degrees C). Grease a 7x11 inch baking dish. Set aside.

### Step 2

Combine raisins, carrots, and water in a medium saucepan. Bring to a boil, reduce heat and simmer for 10 minutes. Remove from heat and allow to cool.

### Step 3

In a mixing bowl, combine flour, oatmeal, sugar substitute, salt, baking soda and cinnamon.

### Step 4

In a separate bowl, mix together the margarine, egg substitute, and vanilla. Add to the flour mixture and mix well.

### Step 5

Add the raisin mixture and nuts, mix well and pour into baking pan.

**Step 6**

Bake for 35 minutes or until toothpick inserted in middle comes out clean.

**Nutrition Facts**

**Per Serving:**

157.5 calories; protein 3.2g 6% DV; carbohydrates 18.5g 6% DV; fat 8.3g 13% DV; cholesterolmg; sodium 242.3mg 10% DV.

# Santa Favorite Cake

**Prep:** 45 mins **Cook:** 25 mins **Additional:** 1 hr **Total:** 2 hrs 10 mins **Servings:** 12 **Yield:** 1 - 3 layer cake

**Ingredients**

- 1 (18.25 ounce) package white cake mix
- 3 large egg whites egg whites
- 1 ⅓ cups buttermilk
- 2 tablespoons vegetable oil
- 1 (9 ounce) package yellow cake mix
- ½ cup buttermilk
- 1 egg

- 1 ½ tablespoons unsweetened cocoa powder
- 2 tablespoons red food coloring
- 1 teaspoon cider vinegar
- 1 (8 ounce) package cream cheese, softened
- 1 cup margarine, softened
- 2 (16 ounce) packages confectioners' sugar
- 2 teaspoons peppermint extract

**Directions**

**Step 1**

Preheat oven to 350 degrees F (175 degrees C). Grease and flour three 9 inch round cake pans.

**Step 2**

In a large bowl, combine white cake mix, 3 egg whites, 1 1/3 cups buttermilk, and 2 tablespoons vegetable oil. Mix with an electric mixer for 2 minutes on high speed. In a separate bowl, combine yellow cake mix, 1/2 cup buttermilk, 1 egg, cocoa, red food coloring, and vinegar. Use an electric mixer to beat for 2 minutes on high speed.

**Step 3**

Spoon white batter alternately with red batter into the prepared cake pans. Swirl batter gently with a knife to create a marbled effect.

**Step 4**

Bake in preheated oven for 22 to 25 minutes, or until a wooden pick inserted into the centers comes out clean. Let cool in pans for at least 10 minutes before turning out onto a wire rack to cool completely.

**Step 5**

In a large bowl, beat cream cheese and margarine until smooth. Gradually blend in sugar until incorporated and smooth. Stir in peppermint extract. Spread peppermint cream cheese frosting between layers, and on top and sides of cake.

**Nutrition Facts**

**Per Serving:**

809.8 calories; protein 7.2g 14% DV; carbohydrates 126.9g 41% DV; fat 31.7g 49% DV; cholesterol 38mg 13% DV; sodium 711.2mg 28% DV.

Printed in Great Britain
by Amazon

19590822R00099